DISCOVERING CAREERS FOR YOUR FUTURE

science

Second Edition

Ferguson
An imprint of ✓®Facts On File

Discovering Careers for Your Future: Science, Second Edition

Copyright © 2005 by Facts On File, Inc.

All rights reserved. No part of this book may be reproduced or utilized in
any form or by any means, electronic or mechanical, including photocopying,
recording, or by any information storage or retrieval systems, without permission
in writing from the publisher. For information contact

Ferguson
An imprint of Facts On File, Inc.
132 West 31st Street
New York NY 10001

Discovering careers for your future. Science—2nd ed.
  p. cm.
Includes bibliographical references and index.
  ISBN 0-8160-5571-8 (hc: alk. paper)
  1. Science—Vocational guidance—Juvenile literature. I. Title: Science.
  Q147.D57 2004
502'.3—dc22   2004004508

Ferguson books are available at special discounts when purchased in
bulk quantities for businesses, associations, institutions, or sales promotions.
Please call our Special Sales Department in New York at (212) 967-8800 or
(800) 322-8755.

You can find Ferguson on the World Wide Web at http://www.fergpubco.com

Text design by Mary Susan Ryan-Flynn

Printed in the United States of America

EB FOF 10 9 8 7 6 5 4 3 2 1

This book is printed on acid-free paper.

Contents

Introduction 1
Agricultural Scientists 5
Archaeologists 9
Astronomers 13
Biochemists 17
Biologists 21
Botanists 25
Chemists 29
Ecologists 33
Genetic Scientists 37
Geologists 41
Geophysicists 45
Marine Biologists 49
Meteorologists 53
Oceanographers 57
Paleontologists 61
Petrologists 65
Pharmacologists 69
Physicists 73
Soil Scientists 77
Zoologists 81
Glossary 85
Index of Job Titles 89
Browse and Learn More 91

Introduction

You may not have decided yet what you want to be in the future. And you do not have to decide right away. However, you may already know that you like science. Knowing your likes and dislikes is a great way to begin thinking about a career. Do any of the statements below describe you? If so, you may want to begin thinking about what a career in science might mean for you.

___Science is my favorite subject in school.
___I like to do science experiments.
___I like animals/plants/insects.
___I collect rocks.
___I collect specimens to view under my microscope.
___I like to study dinosaurs.
___I spend a lot of time working with my chemistry set.
___I like looking at the stars through my telescope.
___I am concerned about the environment.
___I am fascinated by earthquakes, volcanoes, and tornadoes.
___I am curious about how things work.
___I am good at observing small details.
___I like to solve problems.
___I am good at math.
___I like to take things apart and see if I can put them back together again.
___I like to invent things.

Discovering Careers for Your Future: Science is a book about careers in science, from agricultural scientists to zoologists. Scientists help us learn about our universe. Some scientists make discoveries about the Earth, sky, atmosphere, animals, plants, and people. Other scientists figure out practical ways to use those discoveries to make our lives better.

This book describes many possibilities for future careers in the sciences. Read through it and see how different science careers are connected. For example, if you are interested in animals, you will want to read the chapters on biologists, genetic scientists, marine biologists, and zoologists. If you are interested in nature and earth science, you will want to read the chapters on ecologists, geologists, geophysicists, oceanographers, petrologists, and soil scientists.

What Do Scientists Do?

The first section of each chapter begins with a heading such as "What Astronomers Do" or "What Chemists Do." This section tells what it is like to work at this job. It describes typical responsibilities and assignments. You will find out about working conditions. Which scientists work in laboratories? Which ones work outside in all kinds of weather? What tools and equipment do they use? This section answers all these questions.

How Do I Become a Scientist?

The section called "Education and Training" tells you what schooling you need for employment in each job—a high school diploma, training at a junior college, a college degree, or more. It also talks about on-the-job training that you could expect to receive after you are hired and whether or not you must complete an apprenticeship program.

How Much Do Scientists Earn?

The "Earnings" section gives the average salary figures for the job described in the chapter. These figures provide you with a general idea of how much money people with this job can make. Keep in mind that many people really earn more or less than the amounts given here. Actual salaries depend on many different things, such as the size of the company, the location of the company, and the amount of education, training, and experience you have. Generally, but not always, bigger companies located in major cities pay more than smaller ones in smaller cities and towns, and people with more education, training, and experience earn more. Also remember that these figures are current averages. They will probably be different by the time you are ready to enter the workforce.

What Is the Future of Science Careers?

The "Outlook" section discusses the employment outlook for the career: whether the total number of people employed in this career will increase or decrease in the coming years and whether jobs in this field will be easy or hard to find. The U.S. Department of Labor and this book use terms such as "faster than the average," "about as fast as the average," and "slower than the average" to describe job growth predicted by government data. These predictions are based on economic conditions, the size and makeup of the population, foreign competition, and new technology. Keep in mind that these predictions are general statements. No one knows for sure what the future will be like. Also remember that the employment outlook is a general statement about an industry and does not necessarily apply to everyone. A determined and talented person may be able to find a job in an industry or career with the worst kind of outlook. And a person without ambition and the proper training will find it difficult to find a job in even a booming industry or career field.

Where Can I Find More Information?

Each chapter includes a "For More Info" section. It lists organizations that you can contact to find out more about the field and careers in the field. You will find names, addresses, phone numbers, and websites.

Extras

Every chapter has a few extras. There are photos that show scientists in action. There are sidebars and notes on ways to explore the field, related jobs, fun facts, profiles of people in the field, or lists of websites and books that might be helpful. At the end of the book you will find a glossary, which gives brief definitions of words that relate to education, career training, or employment that you may be unfamiliar with. There is an index of all the job titles mentioned in the book, followed by "Browse and Learn More," which is a list of science books and websites.

It is not too soon to think about your future. We hope you discover several possible career choices in this book. Have fun exploring!

Agricultural Scientists

What Agricultural Scientists Do

Agricultural scientists study plants and animals in their environments. They conduct research in laboratories or in the field. They use the results of their research to increase crop yields and improve the environment. Sometimes they plan and set up programs to test foods, drugs, and other products. They may be in charge of activities and public exhibits at such places as zoos and botanical gardens. Some agricultural scientists teach at colleges and universities or work as advisers to business firms or the government. Others work in technical sales and service jobs for companies that make agricultural products.

The head of a research project is usually someone with a doctoral degree (Ph.D.) in agricultural science. The staff working on the research project can range from students to people with advanced degrees. Many agricultural scientists, wherever they work, concentrate on some type of scientific research, either with a team of scientists or an agricultural engineer.

Agronomists are agricultural scientists who try to find the causes of large-scale food-crop problems. They research plant diseases, pests, and weeds, and they also study soil. Their goal is to improve the nutrition,

Important Dates in U.S. Agricultural History

1793	Eli Whitney invents the cotton gin
1819	Jethro Tull invents iron plow with interchangeable parts
1834	McCormick reaper patented
1842	First grain elevator in United States (Buffalo, N.Y.)
1847	Irrigation used for the first time in United States
1874	Use of barbed-wire fences ends open-range grazing

An agricultural scientist performs a controlled experiment on wheat. (Nigel Cattlin / Photo Researchers, Inc.)

hardiness, and taste of the plants by finding better ways to manage disease and soil conditions on a farm.

Horticulturists study the genes and the physical elements of plants to figure out ways to improve plants. They try to make flowers, vegetables, fruits, and nuts, grow faster, bigger, and more resistant to disease by producing better genetic strains of the plants.

Animal scientists specialize in improving the way animals are housed, bred, and fed. They try to control diseases that farm and pet animals get. Some animal scientists study only dairy cattle and how their eating

Bring Conservation to Your Own Backyard

Conservation practices on agricultural and nonagricultural land help:

- provide food and shelter for birds and other wildlife
- control soil erosion
- cut down on sediment in waterways
- conserve water
- improve water quality
- beautify the landscape

The Natural Resources Conservation Service has a Backyard Conservation campaign. It tells you how you can practice conservation in your own backyard. For free tip sheets and a 28-page booklet on Backyard Conservation, call 1-888-LANDCARE or visit this website: http://www.nrcs.usda.gov/feature/backyard.

habits affect their milk supply. Other scientists study only poultry (chickens, turkeys, and ducks) in order to improve the quality and quantity of the birds' eggs and their overall health.

Education and Training

If you like science and are interested in animals and plants, a career in agricultural science may be for you. When you get to high school, you will have to take courses in English, mathematics, government, and history, as well as biology, chemistry, physics, and any other science courses available. You must also learn basic computer skills, including some programming.

After high school, you will have to go to college to earn a bachelor's degree, which may be enough for some beginning jobs. A Ph.D. is usually required for teaching in a college or university or for directing a research program. You can pursue a Ph.D. after completing four years of college and, depending on the school, several years of graduate work. Many colleges and universities offer agricultural science programs. While earning a Ph.D., you will work on research projects, and you will write a research paper, called a dissertation, on your special area of study. You will also do fieldwork and laboratory research along with your classroom studies.

Earnings

Salaries for agricultural scientists vary, depending on your education, experience, employer, and area of study. The average

EXPLORING

- Joining a Future Farmers of America or 4-H club will give you an opportunity to work with others on agricultural projects, such as raising livestock, poultry, and crops. Contact your county's extension office to learn about research projects in your area.
- Visit zoos, agricultural laboratories, greenhouses, or plant nurseries to explore the many opportunities available to agricultural scientists. You may be able to volunteer at zoos, animal shelters, aquariums, botanical gardens, or museums in your area.

salary for all agricultural scientists is $53,000 a year. Some entry-level technician positions pay $32,000 a year, while research directors (a very advanced position) can earn more than $84,000 a year. Researchers with doctorates earn about $60,000 a year. Most agricultural scientists receive health insurance and retirement benefits.

Outlook

Job growth in the field of agricultural science will be slow over the next 10 years. Those who earn master's degrees and Ph.D.'s will have the most opportunities. Certain fields, such as biotechnology and genetics, will offer more jobs than other agricultural science fields.

FOR MORE INFO

For a free career resource guide, contact
American Society of Agronomy
677 South Segoe Road
Madison, WI 53711
Tel: 608-273-8095
http://www.agronomy.org

Visit the USDA website for more information on its agencies and programs as well as news releases.
United States Department of Agriculture (USDA)
http://www.usda.gov

Archaeologists

What Archaeologists Do

Archaeologists study the physical evidence of people who lived in ancient times. They dig up, or excavate, the remains of ancient settlements. These objects can be tools, clay pottery, clothing, weapons, ornaments, and human and animal remains. Archaeologists identify and study these artifacts to learn more about what life was like in the past.

Archaeologists often travel to places where ancient cultures once flourished. At the archaeological site they carefully dig up any objects (*artifacts*) or remains of people, plants, and animals (*realia*) from the culture. They try to clean, repair, and restore the artifacts as nearly as possible to their original condition. They study the realia to figure out what they looked like, what the people ate, how and where they lived, and how they survived.

Archaeologists must keep careful records. They must document exactly where each item was found and what its

Visual Archaeology

In our fast-paced society, even artifacts from the recent past can be lost easily. With that in mind, Frank Jump has climbed walls and crawled over fences to photograph the old painted advertisements fading from the walls of the buildings of New York City. These images, which he calls *visual archaeology*, feature ads for candy bars, bobby pins, and Seely shoulder shapes. Some ads have faded partially to reveal other ads, creating multiple images. The photos have been exhibited at the New York Historical Society and can be seen on the following website: http://www.archaeology.org/online/features/ads/index.html

EXPLORING

- Scouting troops and other youth organizations often go exploring on camping trips.
- Visit nearby museums to see archaeological exhibits. Listen to lectures and talk to museum archaeologists to find out more about archaeology as a career.

condition was. This can be very tedious work. When an archaeology team excavates an area, they brush the layer of dirt off one inch at a time with paint brushes, toothbrushes, and soft bristles. They save all the sand and dirt that they have brushed away. Another member of the team sifts this dirt with a fine screen to find any tiny bone fragments or chips of pottery.

In addition to research, archaeologists teach in colleges or universities or work in museums. Teachers give lectures, correct papers, and take students on field trips. Museum workers may also give lectures, as well as plan museum exhibits and work with the rest of the museum staff.

Education and Training

Becoming an archaeologist involves years of study. In high school, you should study as many modern and foreign languages as possible. Classes in English, writing, history, and social studies will be most helpful. A bachelor's degree is the minimum study after high school. Most archaeologists have also earned a doctorate (Ph.D.). If you want to be an archaeologist, you should enjoy reading, studying, and writing, and have a strong interest in history.

Earnings

As a group, archaeologists and anthropologists make an average salary of $43,000 a year. Archaeologists who work as professors earn an average salary of $67,000 a year. Experienced

Mummified Pets

If you think the ancient Egyptians only mummified humans, think again. Animals were a very important part of ancient Egyptian culture and were mummified regularly. Many of the Egyptians' gods were associated with certain animals, and people would mummify these animals and bury them as an offering to a god. For example, cats were often mummified and offered to the cat goddess Bastet in the hopes that she would provide good health. The Egyptians also mummified falcons by the millions as offerings to Horus, the falcon god, who was believed to cure certain diseases. However, some archaeologists recently X-rayed falcon mummies only to find that there was no bird beneath all of the wrappings. These findings are proof that mummification was a big business in ancient Egypt. Some unsuspecting buyers were obviously fooled into thinking they had purchased a real mummified animal to offer to the gods.

Source: Bob Brier, *dig* magazine online, http://www.digonsite.com

archaeologists who do not work at colleges and universities earn annual salaries between $39,000 and $67,000 a year.

FOR MORE INFO

You can find valuable information about archaeology careers, contact
Archaeological Institute of America
656 Beacon Street
Boston, MA 02215
Tel: 617-353-6550
http://www.archaeological.org

To learn more about the field of archaeology in general, visit
Society for American Archaeology
900 2nd Street NE, Suite 12
Washington, DC 20002
Tel: 202-789-8200
http://www.saa.org

Outlook

Most archaeologists work for colleges and universities, but in the future, there will be fewer teaching jobs available. Job opportunities for archaeologists will be best in research companies, government agencies, and large corporations. The fields of environmental protection and historical preservation are growing, providing more jobs for archaeologists.

Astronomers

What Astronomers Do

Astronomers study the universe and all the celestial, or cosmic, bodies in space. They use telescopes, computers, and complex measuring tools to find the positions of stars and planets. They calculate the orbits of comets, asteroids, and artificial satellites. They study how celestial objects form and deteriorate, and they try to figure out how the universe started.

With special equipment, astronomers collect and analyze information about planets and stars, such as temperature, shape, size, brightness, and motion. They use this knowledge to help scientists know when to launch a space vehicle or a satellite. The astronomer's work also helps other scientists to better understand space, the origins of the Earth and the universe, and the atmosphere surrounding Earth.

Because the field of astronomy is so broad, astronomers usually specialize in one area. For example, *stellar astronomers* study the stars. *Solar astronomers* study the sun. *Planetary astronomers* study conditions on the planets. *Cosmologists* study the origin and the structure of the universe, and *astrophysicists* study the physical and chemical changes that happen in the universe. *Celestial mechanics specialists* study the motion and position of planets and other objects in the solar system. *Radio astronomers* study the source and nature of celestial radio waves using sensitive radio telescopes.

> **NASAKids**
>
> NASA, the National Aeronautics and Space Administration, has a website especially for kids. You can learn about Earth and the other planets, space travel, the stars and galaxies, and NASA. You can even see a launch online. Here's the address: http://kids.mfsc.nasa.gov

An astronomer prepares his telescopes so he can observe a lunar eclipse. (Gregory G. Dimijian / Photo Researchers, Inc.)

Most astronomers teach at universities or colleges. A few lecture at planetariums and teach classes for the public. Some work at research institutions or at observatories. Those who work at observatories spend three to six nights a month observing the night sky through a telescope. They spend the rest of their time in offices or laboratories where they study, analyze their data, and write reports. Other astronomers work

Will Asteroids Strike Earth?

Earth and all the other planets and moons have been continuously hit by asteroids and comets. Craters on the moon are evidence of those strikes. Some people believe an asteroid or comet could strike Earth and cause a disaster. But how likely is this? Astronomers and other scientists say such an event is not very likely. The most dangerous asteroids, those capable of causing major disasters, are extremely rare, according to NASA. These objects hit Earth once every 100,000 years on average.

for government agencies or private industry.

Education and Training

Training to become an astronomer can begin in high school. You should plan to take classes in mathematics, chemistry, physics, geography, and foreign languages (especially French, German, and Russian). Because astronomy is a high-technology field, you should try to learn as much as you can about computers.

In college you will have to earn a bachelor's degree in physics, mathematics, or astronomy. Once you receive your bachelor's degree, you may find work as an assistant or researcher. Most astronomers go on to earn both a master's degree and a doctorate (Ph.D.).

Much of an astronomer's work requires intense concentration. You will spend long hours waiting, observing, and recording data that may not show results right away. But the work is satisfying because astronomers know that the research will help others to learn more about Earth and the universe.

EXPLORING

- Join an amateur astronomy club. There are many such clubs all over the country. These clubs usually have telescopes and will let members of the public view the night skies.
- Visit a nearby planetarium and ask astronomers who work there about their jobs. Planetariums also help you learn more about the universe and see if this is a career you would like.
- There are many astronomy sites on the Internet. Visit the National Aeronautics and Space Administration (NASA) website at http://www.nasa.gov for information on astronomy and links to other astronomy sites. Also check out *Astronomy Magazine* online at http://www.astronomy.com.

Earnings

Astronomers earn an average salary of $80,000 a year. Professors at colleges or universities earn between $30,000 and $68,000 a year, depending on their level of experience and degrees held. Salaries for astronomers who work for the government are usually higher than for astronomers in teaching or observatory positions. The average salary for space professionals (which includes astronomers) working for the federal government is $89,000.

Outlook

Astronomy is one of the smallest science fields, so people trained in astronomy must compete with many others for the best jobs. Many astronomers find jobs in universities and government agencies, but the number of these jobs is not expected to grow in the coming years. The greatest growth in the field of astronomy will be in jobs in business and industry. These jobs may include, for example, helping a company that makes aerospace equipment.

FOR MORE INFO

For more information about a career in astronomy, contact the following:

American Astronomical Society
2000 Florida Avenue, Suite 400
Washington, DC 20009
Tel: 202-328-2010
http://www.aas.org

American Institute of Physics
One Physics Ellipse
College Park, MD 20740
Tel: 301-209-3100
http://www.aip.org

Amateur Astronomers Association of New York
1010 Park Avenue
New York, NY 10028
Tel: 212-535-2922
http://www.aaa.org

Biochemists

What Biochemists Do

Biochemists study the chemical makeup of plants and animals. They try to understand how chemical makeup affects the way living things grow and develop. Sometimes they look at how changes in the environment affect the materials found in living cells. They also study how plants and animals inherit certain characteristics.

Some biochemists can work in biotechnology, which means that they design and create new types of plants and chemicals. If they know that one type of chemical is close to what they need for a specific purpose, they can try to change the structure of the chemical to make it work. Or they can try to get a plant to produce the chemical they need.

Some biochemists work in the field of medicine, where they investigate the causes and cures of disease. Others experiment with changing the structure of living cells to create artificial chemicals to treat disease and infection. Their area of study is called biomedicine.

Some biochemists study nutrition. They examine the effects of eating habits on a person's ability to learn and remain healthy, for example. Biochemists also work in agriculture, where they try to discover better

> **Words to Learn**
>
> **atom** the smallest part of anything in the world; has a proton and a neutron in its center, called a nucleus; electrons spin around the nucleus
> **atomic mass** total mass of all the atom's parts
> **atomic number** number of protons and electrons in a neutral atom
> **carbohydrates** sugars that provide living things with energy
> **lipids** type of organic molecule; fats, steroids, and waxes are lipids

EXPLORING

- Read science and medical magazines to help you learn more about recent breakthroughs in the biochemistry field.
- Visit science museums in your area.
- Practice using a microscope and make detailed notes and diagrams of what you see.

ways to grow and store crops and keep them free from disease.

Most biochemists use powerful electron microscopes to magnify tiny particles. But they also have developed new instruments that follow the action of the chemicals they are studying.

Biochemists usually work in clean, quiet, well-lighted laboratories. They often work alone for long periods of time on projects that do not give them results right away. Some biochemists try to prove scientific theories or make new discoveries. This is called basic research. Others work on projects that use basic research to solve specific problems. This is called

Who Discovered Cells?

Robert Hooke, an English scientist, first described and named cells in 1665, when he looked at a slice of bark from an oak tree under a microscope with a magnifying power of 30x. Hooke never realized the importance of his discovery, however. He thought the tiny boxes or "cells" he saw were unique to the bark. Anton van Leeuwenhoek, a Dutch scientist who lived in Hooke's time, discovered single-celled organisms by observing them in pond water and in animal blood. He used grains of sand that he had polished into magnifying glasses as powerful as 300x to see this invisible world. In 1839, nearly two centuries after Hooke's and Leeuwenhoek's discoveries, two German biologists, Matthias Schleiden and Theodor Schwann, correctly concluded that all living things consisted of cells.

applied research because theories and discoveries are immediately applied to create, for example, a new drug, or to grow crops that resist disease.

Education and Training

In high school, take as many math, science, and computer courses as you can to prepare for this career. In college, you must earn a bachelor's degree with a major in biochemistry, chemistry, or biology to pursue work in this field. With a bachelor's degree, you could find a job as a research assistant in a drug laboratory. A bachelor's degree could also qualify you for a job as a technician or technologist in biochemistry or another field related to the biological sciences.

To get a more advanced position in research, you will need at least a master's degree. For the most advanced positions, for example, as a university professor or director of a research project, a doctorate (Ph.D.) is required.

Earnings

Biochemists make an average salary of $66,000 a year. The average income for entry-level jobs in biochemistry is about $30,000 a year. Biochemists employed in private industry earn an average of $50,000. Some biochemists with advanced degrees and a good deal of experience can earn more than $90,000 a year in industry or government jobs. Biochemists who start out working for the federal government, however, can expect to earn slightly less than those who get jobs in private industry or in colleges or universities.

Outlook

There will be good opportunities for jobs in biochemistry through 2012, especially in medical research. Biochemists are trying to find cures for such diseases as AIDS, cancer, and mental illness. Finding better ways to protect the environment from pollution has also created jobs for biochemists.

FOR MORE INFO

For more information about careers, education, and scholarships, contact the following:

American Chemical Society
1155 16th Street, NW
Washington, DC 20036
Tel: 800-227-5558
http://www.chemistry.org

American Institute of Biological Sciences
1441 I Street, NW Suite 200
Washington, DC 20005
Tel: 202-628-1500
http://www.aibs.org

American Society for Biochemistry and Molecular Biology
Education Information
9650 Rockville Pike
Bethesda, MD 20814-3996
Tel: 301-634-7145
http://www.asbmb.org

Biologists

What Biologists Do

Biologists study how plants and animals grow and reproduce. Sometimes called *biological scientists* or *life scientists*, they often have other job titles because they specialize in one area of biology. *Botanists*, for example, study different types of plants. *Zoologists* study different types of animals. Biologists study living things, while chemists, physicists, and geologists study nonliving matter like rocks and chemicals.

Biologists may do their research in the field or in the laboratory. Their exact job responsibilities vary depending on their area of interest. For example, *aquatic biologists* study plants and animals that live in water. They may do much of their research on a boat studying the water temperature, amount of light, salt levels, and other environmental conditions in the ocean. They then observe how fish and other plants and animals react to these environments.

No matter what type of research biologists do, they must keep careful records to note all procedures and results. Because biologists may sometimes work with dangerous chemicals and other materials, they always must take safety precautions and carefully follow each step in an experiment.

Activities for Budding Biologists

If you enjoy one of the following activities, you may have a future as a biologist:
- bird watching
- collecting butterflies and other insects
- gardening
- microscope study
- raising or caring for animals
- watching nature shows
- visiting nature preserves
- going to the zoo

Some biologists advise businesses and governmental agencies. Others inspect foods and other products. Many biologists write articles for scientific journals. Some may also teach at schools or universities.

Education and Training

If you are thinking about a career in biology, you should plan to take high school courses in biology, chemistry, mathematics, physics, and a foreign language. After high school, you must obtain a bachelor's degree in biology. During college, you will take more advanced courses in biology, math, chemistry, and physics. Then you choose a specialty, such as microbiology, bacteriology, botany, ecology, or anatomy. Most successful biologists also have a master's degree or a doctorate (Ph.D.) in biology or in a related field.

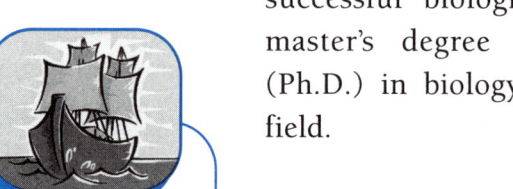

EXPLORING

- You can learn about the work of biologists at school field trips to federal private laboratories and research centers.
- Visit your local museums of natural history or science, aquariums, and zoos.
- Many park districts offer classes and field trips to help you explore plant and animal life.
- Take science courses that offer laboratory time, such as biology, chemistry, and physics, to see how you like working in that environment.

Earnings

The average salary for a biologist ranges from $30,000 to more than $70,000 a year. Biologists who specialize in one area, such as botany or ecology, tend to earn higher salaries. Government biologists earn an average salary of about $62,000 a year.

Outlook

There should be plenty of jobs for skilled biologists in the next decade. There are many people competing for jobs in biology, so

What Microbiologists Do

Microbiologists are scientists who study bacteria, viruses, molds, algae, yeasts, and other organisms of microscopic size. They study the form and structure of these microorganisms, how they reproduce, and how they affect other living things, such as humans, animals, and plants. Microbiologists work in laboratories at universities, research facilities, and medical institutions, such as hospitals.

Medical microbiologists diagnose, treat, and prevent disease. They use blood and tissue samples from patients to try and find the microbes that cause illness; these microbes are called pathogens. Clinical microbiologists also try to diagnose and prevent disease. Microbiologists' research has helped to prevent the spread of many diseases, including typhoid fever, influenza, measles, polio, whooping cough, and smallpox. Today, microbiologists are trying to find cures for such diseases as AIDS, cancer, cystic fibrosis, and Alzheimer's disease.

Many microbiologists work in the food industry. They identify pathogens in restaurant kitchens or in processed food that cause salmonella food poisoning. Microbiologists have identified many microorganisms that are useful to humans. These tiny organisms have been used in the making of food, such as cheese, bread, and tofu. Other microorganisms are used to preserve food and tenderize meat. Flavors, colors, and added vitamins are all made from microbes.

Microbiologists also work in industry. They make sure manufactured goods are safe. In the pharmaceutical industry, they develop new drugs, such as antibiotics. Microbiologists also test new drugs and cosmetics. They develop new products, such as biological washing detergents. Some microbiologists work for water companies or environmental agencies. They test the quality of water.

those with the most education and training will have the best chances at being hired.

FOR MORE INFO

For information about a career as a biologist, contact
American Institute of Biological Sciences
1444 I Street, NW, Suite 200
Washington, DC 20005
Tel: 202-628-1500
http://www.aibs.org

For a career brochure and career-related articles, contact
American Physiological Society
Education Office
9650 Rockville Pike
Bethesda, MD 20814
Tel: 301-634-7164
http://www.the-aps.org

For information on careers and educational resources, contact
American Society for Microbiology
Office of Education and Training—Career Information
1752 N Street, NW
Washington, DC 20036
Tel: 202-737-3600
http://www.asm.org

For career information, including articles and books, contact
Biotechnology Industry Organization
1225 I Street, NW, Suite 400
Washington, DC 20005
Tel: 202-962-9200
http://www.bio.org

Botanists

What Botanists Do

Botanists study plants, including cell structure; how plants reproduce; how plants are distributed on Earth; and how rainfall, climate, and other conditions affect them.

Botany is a major branch of biology. Botanists play an important part in modern science and industry. Their work affects agriculture, agronomy (soil and crop science), conservation, forestry, and horticulture. Botanists develop new drugs to treat disease. They find more food resources for developing countries. They discover solutions to environmental problems.

Botanists who specialize in agriculture or agronomy try to develop new varieties of crops that are more resistant to disease. Or they may try to improve the growth of crops such as high-yield corn. These botanists focus on a specific type of plant species, such as ferns (pteridology), or plants that are

---

It's a Bug's Life

Though many bugs are harmful to plants, some can be beneficial. These bugs prey on plant-feeding insects, and it isn't pretty—the following scenes of violence may not be suitable for all readers!

- Ladybugs eat aphids, mealy bugs, and mites. Adults may eat 50 or more aphids a day.
- Praying mantis kill their plant-feeding prey by biting the back of the neck, severing the main nerves.
- Lacewings suck the body fluids from their prey and carry the remains of their victims on their backs.
- Hover flies grasp plant-feeding insects and puncture them using tiny hooks in their mouths.

native to a specific area, such as wetland or desert. Botanists who work in private industry, such as a food or drug company, may focus on developing new products, or they may test and inspect products.

Research botanists work at research stations at colleges and universities and botanical gardens. Botanists who work in conservation or ecology often do their work out in the field. They help recreate lost or damaged ecosystems, direct pollution cleanups and take inventories of species.

There are many specialties in botany. *Ethnobotanists* study how a particular culture or ethnic group uses plants to treat diseases and injuries. *Ecologists* study the connection between plants and animals and the physical environment. They restore native species to areas, repair damaged ecosystems, and work on pollution problems. *Forest ecologists* focus on forest species and their habitats, such as forest wetlands. *Mycologists* study fungi and apply their findings to medicine, agriculture, and industry. *Plant cytologists* use powerful microscopes to study plant tissues to find out why some cells cause the plant to get sick or die. *Plant geneticists* study the origin and development of inherited traits, such as size and color. *Toxicologists* study the effect of toxic substances on organisms, including plants. Results of their work may be used in new laws, product labeling, and other areas.

EXPLORING

- Take part in science fairs and clubs.
- Volunteer to work for parks, nurseries, farms, labs, camps, florists, or landscape architects.
- Tour a botanical garden in your area and talk to staff.
- Grow your own garden, including fruits and vegetables, herbs, flowers, and indoor plants. Keep a notebook to record how each plant responds to watering, fertilizing, and sunlight.
- Hobbies like camping, photography, and computers are useful, too.

Education and Training

In high school, college-preparatory courses in math, biology, chemistry, and computers are good preparation

What Horticultural Technicians Do

Horticultural technicians grow and sell plants and flowers that make our surroundings more beautiful. They work with flowers, shrubs, trees, and grass. Horticultural technicians plant and care for grass and trees in parks, on playgrounds, and along public highways. There are nearly 1 million people employed in landscape and horticultural services.

Horticultural technicians usually specialize in one of the following areas: floriculture (flowers), nursery operation (shrubs, hedges, and trees), turfgrass (grass), and arboriculture (trees).

Technicians plant seeds; transplant seedlings; inspect crops for nutrient deficiencies, insects, diseases, and unwanted plant growth; remove substandard plants; and prune other plants. Horticultural technicians feed nutrients to plants and flowers. They regulate humidity, ventilation, and carbon dioxide conditions. They use herbicides, fungicides, and pesticides to protect plants.

for this career. If you want to become a botanist, you will have to go to college and earn a bachelor's degree. For research and teaching positions, you will have to go on to earn a master's or even a doctorate (Ph.D.). These higher degrees require you to specialize in one of the many specialized areas in botany. For example, a master's in conservation biology focuses on the conservation of specific plant and animal communities.

Earnings

Graduates with bachelor's degrees in biological sciences such as botany start out earning about $30,000 a year. Botanists with master's degrees make an average starting salary of $35,000 a year, and those with Ph.D.'s make an average starting salary of $43,000. Botanists and other biological scientists working for the federal government make an average salary of $62,000 a year.

Outlook

Employment for botanists is expected to increase faster than the average in the next decade. Botanists will be needed to help with environmental, conservation, and pharmaceutical issues. Botanists work in such a wide variety of fields that some type of employment is almost guaranteed for someone with a degree in this field. Opportunities will be best for those with advanced degrees.

FOR MORE INFO

Contact the following organization for information about careers in botany:

Botanical Society of America
PO Box 299
St. Louis, MO 63166
Tel: 314-577-9566
http://www.botany.org

Contact this group about volunteer positions in natural resource management:

Student Conservation Association
689 River Road
PO Box 55
Charlestown, NH 03603
Tel: 603-543-1700
http://www.the-sca.org

Chemists

What Chemists Do

Chemistry is the study of the physical and chemical properties of matter. *Chemists* improve products and create new ones, such as drugs, synthetic plastics and fabrics, rocket fuels for space travel, and light metals such as aluminum, magnesium, and titanium.

Food chemists develop new foods and try to make them stay fresh longer. They study how methods of cooking, canning, freezing, and packaging affect the taste, appearance, and quality of different food products. They test samples of meats, cereals, and dairy products to make sure that they meet government food standards.

Analytical chemists study the composition of substances and analyze them. They set standards for safe levels of certain chemicals in drinking water and also examine wastewater from industrial plants for pollutants. Physical chemists study atoms and molecules to predict how they will behave under a variety of reaction conditions. *Toxicologists* study the by-products produced by paint, petroleum, leather,

Safety First

Chemists are exposed to dangerous materials as they work. They follow safety precautions in everything they do. Be sure to adopt these safety guidelines when you conduct any kind of experiment:

- Always work with an adult.
- Wear protective eyewear.
- Read and follow all directions carefully.
- Wear gloves and tie back your hair if it is long.
- Keep all materials away from your nose and eyes.
- Never eat or drink while experimenting.
- Wash your hands thoroughly when you are finished.
- Maintain a clean work area at all times.

Most chemists spend their time in a laboratory conducting experiments. (digitalvision)

and pharmaceutical manufacturers. They design ways to prevent harmful effects on users of the products and on the environment.

Education and Training

Training for a career in chemistry begins in high school. You should take at least three or four years of mathematics, including algebra, geometry, and calculus; three years of science, including biology, chemistry, and physics; and four years of English. Computer classes are also important.

After high school, you must go to college to earn a bachelor's degree, which is enough for an entry-level job. Higher level jobs require more education. To become a researcher in

EXPLORING

- Ask your teacher to help you with chemistry experiments.
- There are junior chemistry sets available that teach you about the scientific method, how to perform chemical experiments, and chemical words and phrases.
- Your school librarian can help you find chemistry books and computer programs.

> ## What Chemical Technicians Do
>
> *Chemical technicians* who work in the chemical industry develop, test, and manufacture plastics, paints, detergents, synthetic fibers, industrial chemicals, and pharmaceuticals. Others work in the petroleum, aerospace, metals, electronics, automotive, and construction industries.
>
> *Laboratory testing technicians* work in all kinds of laboratories in industries such as electronics, aerospace, oil, automobile, and construction companies. They use tools and instruments to conduct tests on substances and products to see that they meet specifications and performance standards.
>
> To be a chemical technician, you must complete a two-year chemical technology program at a community college. Chemical technicians who have completed a two-year training program earn about $21,000 a year to start. Experienced technicians earn an average salary of $38,000 a year.
>
> The pharmaceutical industry will have the greatest need for chemical technicians in the future. The consumer goods, metallurgical, and industrial-products industries will continue to hire chemical testing technicians in good numbers. Overall, the number of opportunities for all technicians will be excellent.

industry, a master's degree or a doctorate (Ph.D.) is necessary. Almost all college and university research and teaching positions require a doctorate.

Earnings

Chemists' salaries depend on ability, education, experience, the nature of the job, and where you work. The average salary for all chemists is $58,000 a year. The average starting salary for a chemist with a bachelor's degree and no experience in private industry is about $30,000 a year. With a master's degree, the starting salary is about $38,000 a year. An experienced chemist with a Ph.D. and supervisory duties can earn $90,000 a year or more.

Outlook

Chemists who develop new products for private industry will find the most opportunities for jobs in the next decade. Most openings will be in pharmaceuticals, biotechnology, and firms that produce specialty chemicals. As with many science fields, job candidates with advanced degrees, especially doctorates, will be eligible for the highest paying jobs.

FOR MORE INFO

For more information about a career as a chemist, contact the following organizations:

American Chemical Society (ACS)
Department of Career Services
1155 16th Street, NW
Washington, DC 20036
Tel: 800-227-5558
http://www.chemistry.org

American Institute of Chemists (AIC)
315 Chestnut Street
Philadelphia, PA 19106
Tel: 215-873-8224
http://www.theaic.org

Chemical Institute of Canada (CIC)
130 Slater Street, Suite 550
Ottawa, Ontario, Canada K1P 6E2
Tel: 888-542-2242
http://www.cheminst.ca

Ecologists

What Ecologists Do

Ecologists study how plants and animals live in their environments. They find out how pollutants, rainfall, temperature, and altitude affect living things. For example, an ecologist may compare the differences and similarities between clean and polluted rivers. They may study how a forest recovers after a fire.

Some ecologists specialize. For example, *forest ecologists* research how changes in the environment affect forests. They may study what causes a certain type of tree to grow abundantly, including light and soil requirements and resistance to insects and disease. Another type of ecologist is the *hydrogeologist*, who studies waters on or below the surface of the earth. *Geochemists* study the chemistry of the earth, including the effects of pollution on that chemistry.

Ecologists study plants and animals both in natural settings and in the laboratory. They use electron microscopes, electronic instruments, computers, and other equipment. When working outdoors, ecologists may live in remote areas under

> **Words to Learn**
>
> **canopy** upper layer of a forest, created by the foliage and branches of the tallest trees
>
> **coniferous** trees that bear cones
>
> **ecosystem** community of animals and plants and their interaction with the environment
>
> **effluent** wastewater or sewage that flows into a river, lake, or ocean
>
> **riparian zone** forest or grass growing on the banks of a stream; the riparian zone can prevent soil erosion
>
> **savanna** flat, grassy plain found in tropical areas
>
> **tundra** cold region where the soil under the surface of the ground is permanently frozen
>
> **watershed** gathering ground of a river system, a ridge that separates two river basins, or an area of land that slopes into a river or lake

> ### The Evolution of Ecology
>
> The term *ecology* was first defined in 1866 by Ernst von Haeckel, a German biologist. He grappled with Charles Darwin's theory of evolution based on natural selection. This theory said that those species of plants and animals that were best adapted to their environment would survive. Haeckel did not agree with Darwin, but he and many other scientists were fascinated with the links between living things and their physical environment. Recognizing that there was such a link was a key step in the development of the science of ecology.
>
> Like most of the other environmental careers, the professional field of ecology did not really grow popular until the late 1960s and early 1970s, when the U.S. government passed a series of hard-hitting environmental laws. These laws regulated, among other things, the ways in which large companies manufactured and disposed of materials. At first companies looked to professionals in existing science and engineering fields to help them comply with the new laws, but everyone soon realized the research needed in this field called for dedicated specialists. Thus, ecologists became a new and much needed group of professionals.

rough conditions. Their work may involve strenuous physical activity.

The study of ecology helps protect, clean, improve, and preserve our environment. Ecologists investigate industry and government actions and help correct past environmental problems. Sometimes they work with dangerous organisms or toxic substances in the laboratory.

Education and Training

To be an ecologist you must go to college and earn a bachelor of science degree in biology, chemistry, botany, zoology, or another science. You must be able to work on your own or as part of a team. You must have good writing skills, which are important for writing reports. Physical strength is necessary for some field work. For research or management jobs you will also need a master's degree. For higher positions, such as college professor or research supervisor, you need a doctorate (Ph.D.).

Earnings

The average salary for all environmental scientists, including ecologists, is about $50,000 a year. With experience and a Ph.D., you can earn

EXPLORING

- Join a scouting organization or environmental protection group to gain firsthand experience in the work of an ecologist.
- Visit natural history museums.
- Visit nearby parks or forest preserves. What kinds of trees and plants grow there? Which insects, animals and birds are native to the area?

FOR MORE INFO

For more information about a career as an ecologist, contact the following organizations:

American Geological Institute
4220 King Street
Alexandria, VA 22302
Tel: 703-379-2480
http://www.agiweb.org

Ecological Society of America
1707 H Street, NW
Suite 400
Washington, DC 20006
Tel: 202-833-8773
http://www.esa.org

For information on student volunteer activities, contact

Student Conservation Association
689 River Road
PO Box 550
Charlestown, NH 03603
Tel: 603-543-1700
http://www.the-sca.org

For information on careers, publications, and internships, contact

Environmental Careers Organization
30 Winter Street
Boston, MA 02108
Tel: 617-426-4375
http://www.eco.org

$85,000 or more. Most private companies pay higher salaries than the federal government.

Outlook

The job outlook for environmental workers in general should be faster than average over the next decade. But there will be fewer jobs in land and water conservation. This is because so many ecologists compete for these popular jobs. Those with advanced degrees will have the best chances for employment.

Genetic Scientists

What Genetic Scientists Do

Genetic scientists, or *geneticists,* study heredity, or how certain traits are passed from one generation to the next. Genetic research helps us understand a wide range of issues, from preventing or controlling some diseases to breeding new crops and livestock. Geneticists manipulate or alter an organism's genetic characteristics to better understand how genetic systems work. For instance, a genetic scientist may breed a family of mice with a tendency toward high blood pressure to test the effects of exercise or diet on that condition.

With the many advances that have occurred in genetics, genetic scientists have a wider range of opportunities than ever before. After several years of supervised research and study, *research geneticists* usually work on the faculty of a university or for biotechnology firms. *Laboratory geneticists* apply genetics to agriculture, police work, pharmaceutical development,

---

Monks and Peas

Gregor Mendel (1822–84) was an Austrian monk with a keen interest in plants and science. By performing many experiments with pea plants, Mendel observed that certain combinations of plants with different traits (such as differences in height) yielded predictable traits in the next generation of plants. These traits, Mendel determined, resulted from different combination of hereditary units, called *genes,* which plants received from their parents. Mendel believed these discoveries could be applied to all living things. Although his findings were mostly ignored in his lifetime, Mendel's theories became the scientific laws governing genetics and are still in use today.

and medicine. *Clinical geneticists* are generally medical doctors who are highly specialized in the field of genetics. *Genetic counselors* work in health care with people who may be at risk for inherited conditions or who may have family members with birth defects or genetic disorders. *Genetic engineers* alter, splice, and rearrange genes for specific results, such as for cloning experiments or medical advancements.

Most geneticists spend their time working in a laboratory. They work with chemicals, heat, light, and such instruments as microscopes, computers, electron microscopes, and other technical equipment. Geneticists must have excellent analytical and mathematical skills to perform their research. They must be able to communicate their findings clearly in classrooms and in written reports.

Education and Training

High school courses in math, biology, chemistry, physics, and computers will help you prepare for a career in genetics. A bachelor's degree in biology, genetics, or a physical science is a must for this profession. Most genetic scientists also hold advanced degrees. For example, most research geneticists who teach at a college level hold a doctorate (Ph.D.). Clinical geneticists usually attend medical school after completing college. Many geneticists working for large corporations, making everything from medicine to microchips, hold master's degrees. Genetic counselors go through master's programs that focus on medical genetics and counseling.

EXPLORING

- Arrange a visit with a department of genetics or biology at a local college.
- Trace the history of a certain trait, like eye color, in your family.
- Read about the work of famous geneticists, such as Gregor Mendel, James Watson, and Francis Crick.

Dolly

In 1997, the birth of a sheep in Scotland became one of the biggest news stories in the history of science. This is because the sheep, Dolly, was no ordinary animal. She was a clone, an exact genetic duplicate, of another adult sheep.

Unlike other sheep, who have two parents, Dolly was created in a laboratory from the genetic materials from the cells of an adult sheep. Although scientists had previously succeeded in cloning embryonic (or unborn) sheep—a pair of twins named Morag and Megan—no one had been successful in cloning an adult. But a team of genetic scientists led by Dr. Iam Wilmut discovered a way to do it, which involved complex chemical treatments, careful laboratory procedures, and lots of patience.

Dolly's birth was top news around the world. The story made many people wonder if human cloning might soon become a possibility, even though it is illegal in many countries and is the subject of great controversy. After Dolly's birth, President Bill Clinton requested a review of all U.S. research in the area of cloning.

Science magazine named Dolly the top scientific discovery of 1997.

Earnings

Starting salaries for genetic scientists with bachelor's degrees working for the federal government are around $24,000. Genetic scientists with master's degrees start at $30,000–$36,000, depending on their specialty. The average salary for genetic scientists working in private industry is around $55,000, with biotechnology firms offering even higher salaries. The highest paid, most experienced genetic scientists make $70,000–$80,000 or more a year.

Outlook

Because of the many advances in genetic research over the past decade, genetic scientists will experience faster than average job growth in coming years. Since genetic research is useful in so many areas, genetic scientists can find opportunities in almost any field that interests them. Many scientists and engineers consider genetics to be the most promising scientific field today.

FOR MORE INFO

For information about genetics careers, contact

Genetics Society of America
9650 Rockville Pike
Bethesda, MD 20814
Tel: 301-634-7300
http://www.genetics-gsa.org

For information on genetic counseling, contact

National Society of Genetic Counselors
233 Canterbury Drive
Wallingford, PA 19086
Tel: 610-872-7608
http://www.nsgc.org

The following website has links to many genetics societies and websites:
http://www.faseb.org/genetics

Geologists

What Geologists Do

Geologists study the earth—how it was formed, what it is made of, and how it is slowly changing. They take rock samples. Generally, geologists spend three to six months of the year making maps of certain areas and drilling deep holes to obtain these rock samples. They study the rock samples in their laboratories under controlled temperatures and pressures. Finally, they organize the information they have gathered and write reports. These reports may be used to locate groundwater, oil, minerals, and other natural resources.

Many geologists specialize in a particular field of study. For example, those who study the oceans are called *marine geologists*. Those who try to locate natural gas and oil deposits are called *petroleum geologists*. *Paleontologists* study the earth's rock formations to determine the age of the earth.

Rock-Collecting Tips

Many people collect rocks as a hobby. Some gather them for color, such as agate with its bands of many hues. Others collect specimens for odd or beautiful shapes. Some look for imprints of fossils. Some gather historic rocks, such as stones from battlefields or Indian mounds.

For people who want to do their own collecting, every part of the country offers specimens. Mountains, seashores, riverbanks, woods, and lava plains are especially abundant in varied rocks. Many people simply pick up rocks on the surface of the ground. Others carry rock hammers, picks, nippers, and Geiger counters. Hobbyists can buy rocks from specialty stores or scientific supply houses. For more information visit http://www.rocks-rock.com

Geologists' work can be physically demanding. They travel often and spend a lot of time in remote and rugged areas. In addition, they spend long hours in the laboratory and preparing reports.

Most geologists work in private businesses. More than half of them work for oil and gas companies in the field of exploration. The federal government hires geologists to work in the Department of the Interior (the U.S. Geological Survey, the Bureau of Mines, or the Bureau of Reclamation) and in the Departments of Defense, Agriculture, and Commerce. Geologists also work for state agencies, research organizations, universities, and museums.

EXPLORING

- Join a rock collecting club or start one yourself. Amateur geological groups and local museums may have geology clubs.
- Here are some reading suggestions:
  Anderson, Alan. *Geology Crafts for Kids: 50 Nifty Projects to Explore the Marvels of Planet Earth.* New York: Sterling, 1998.
  Hiscock, Bruce. *The Big Rock.* Aladdin Library, 1999.
  National Wildlife Federation. *Geology: The Active Earth.* New York: McGraw-Hill, 1997.

Education and Training

To be a geologist, you will have to go to college and earn a bachelor's degree, usually in the physical and earth sciences. Positions in research, teaching, or exploration require a master's degree. Geologists who want to teach in a college or university or be in charge of a department in a company must earn a doctorate (Ph.D.).

Many colleges, universities, and technical institutes offer programs in geology. Besides courses in geology, students study physics, chemistry, mathematics, English composition, economics, and foreign languages. Students who go on to graduate school will take advanced courses in geology and in the specialization of their choice.

What Geological Technicians Do

Geological technicians help geologists study the Earth's physical makeup and history. This includes the exploration of mountain uplifting, rock formations, mineral deposits, earthquakes, and volcanoes.

Petroleum technicians measure and record the conditions of oil and gas wells. They use instruments lowered into the wells, and evaluate mud from the wells. They examine data to determine petroleum and mineral content.

Geological technicians most often work as part of a research team. They usually work with petroleum geologists, who determine where deposits of oil and natural gas may be buried beneath the earth's surface. Geological technicians draw maps to show where drilling operations are taking place. They write reports that geologists use to determine where an oil deposit might be located. Geological technicians also draw maps that show exactly where a drilling crew has dug a well. The map tells whether or not oil was found and specifies the depth of the well.

Some geological technicians work in the field of environmental engineering. They help geologists study how structures such as roads, landfills, and buildings affect the environment.

Geological technicians need to have a two-year associate's degree. Many technicians earn a bachelor of science degree with an emphasis in geology, mathematics, or drafting. Entry-level geological technicians in private industry earn about $20,000 a year. Those with more experience earn an average of $36,000 a year. Job opportunities for geological technicians depend on the state of the oil and gas industry, but overall the outlook for these jobs is good.

Earnings

Geoscientists, a group that includes geologists, on average make between $67,000 and $79,000 a year. Beginning geologists earn about $33,000 a year. Those with master's and doctoral degrees earn more than those with a bachelor's degree. Geologists who work for the federal government generally earn less.

Outlook

Job opportunities for geologists are good. The petroleum and environmental protection and reclamation industries will offer the most jobs, but competition for those jobs will be stiff. Geologists with advanced degrees, an ability to speak a foreign language, and who are willing to relocate overseas if necessary will have big advantages over other candidates.

FOR MORE INFO

For more information about a career as a geologist, contact the following organizations:

American Geological Institute
4220 King Street
Alexandria, VA 22302
Tel: 703-379-2480
http://www.agiweb.org

The Geological Society of America
PO Box 9140
Boulder, CO 80301
Tel: 888-443-4472
http://www.geosociety.org

Geophysicists

What Geophysicists Do

Geophysics combines the sciences of geology and physics. *Geophysicists* study the physical structure of the earth. This includes land surfaces, underground areas, and bodies of water. They use their knowledge to predict earthquakes, discover oil, and find places to build power plants. Their duties may include fieldwork, laboratory research, or college teaching.

Geophysicists usually specialize in one area of geophysics. For example, *seismologists* study earthquakes. *Hydrologists* study the movement and distribution of water. *Meteorologists* study weather patterns. No matter what their area of specialization, geophysicists use the scientific principles of geology, chemistry, mathematics, physics, and engineering. Many of their instruments, such as the seismograph, take precise

International Geophysical Year

The International Geophysical Year (IGY) was held from July 1, 1957, to December 31, 1958. During the 18-month "year," IGY scientists from 66 nations carried out experiments and observations in all parts of the world. The most spectacular achievement of the IGY was the launching of the first artificial satellites.

After the IGY, scientists studied the information they collected. These are some of the major discoveries.

- The earth bulges about 45 feet at the North Pole.
- The world's climate as a whole is getting warmer.
- The lowest natural temperature that had ever been recorded, -125.3°F, was recorded in Antarctica.
- The amount of ice on Earth is nearly 4,500,000 cubic miles—40 percent more than scientists had estimated before the IGY.

measurements of the earth's physical characteristics, such as its electric, magnetic, and gravitational fields.

Geophysicists often study environmental issues. For example, they may investigate whether an explosion designed to expose rich mineral deposits might also lead to an earthquake. They might examine the quality of underground water and how it affects a city's drinking supply.

Field geophysicists work outdoors in all kinds of weather. They often travel and work in isolated areas.

Education and Training

Geophysicists should have a solid background in mathematics and the physical and earth sciences. In high school you should take four years of mathematics and courses in earth science, physics, and chemistry. Classes in mechanical drawing, history, and English are also recommended.

The best way to become a geophysicist is to get a bachelor's degree in geophysics or geology. A degree in physics, mathematics, or chemistry might be sufficient, but you should also take as many geology courses as you can. You will need a master's degree or doctorate in geology or geophysics for research or college teaching positions, and other positions with good advancement potential.

EXPLORING

- You can find out more about geophysics by reading books on electricity, rocks and minerals, metals and metallurgy, the universe and space, and weather and climate.
- Develop hobbies that deal with radio, electronics, rock collecting, or map collecting.
- Take a look at the Society of Exploration Geophysicists kids' website at http://students.seg.org/kids/

Earnings

The average starting salary for a geophysicist is $33,000 a year. The average mid-range salary is $60,000. Experienced geophysicists with doctorates earn more than $90,000 a year.

> ## Earth-Shattering Facts
>
> - Scientists believe that the San Andreas fault may be 100 million years old. It cuts through the state of California for almost 700 miles. Small earthquakes along the San Andreas fault occur several times a month. Not all earthquakes are dangerous, but many lives have been lost due to earthquakes along the fault. In the 1906 San Francisco earthquake, 500 people died from falling buildings and fires. The city burned for three days.
> - There are over 1 million quakes around the world each year, including those too small to be felt.
> - A magnitude 9.5 earthquake in Chile in 1960 was the largest known earthquake and resulted in over 6,000 deaths. It triggered a tsunami (seismic wave) that killed people as far away as Hawaii and Japan.
> - The great Alaska earthquake of March 27, 1964, was the strongest earthquake in the United States. It had a magnitude of 9.2. Approximately 115 people died, with most of the deaths due to the tsunami it generated. Shaking was felt for an estimated 7 minutes, and raised or lowered the ground surface as much as 56 feet in some areas.
> - Alaska has more earthquakes per year than the combined total of the rest of the United States. As many as 4,000 are recorded there every year.
>
> Source: Center for Earthquake Research and Information, http://www.ceri.memphis.edu

Outlook

Job growth for geophysicists is expected to grow at an average rate over the next 10 years. Many geophysicists will find work in the petroleum as gas industries, where they will be needed to find new deposits of these natural resources. Even if job prospects in the oil and gas industries decline, there will continue to be jobs in teaching and other research areas.

FOR MORE INFO

For more information about a career as a geophysicist, contact

American Geophysical Union
2000 Florida Avenue, NW
Washington, DC 20009
Tel: 202-462-6900
http://www.agu.org

Society of Exploration Geophysicists
PO Box 702740
Tulsa, OK 74170
Tel: 918-497-5500
http://seg.org

Marine Biologists

What Marine Biologists Do

Marine biologists study the plants and animals that live in salt water. They learn about the tens of thousands of different species that make their homes in the ocean.

To study these plants and animals in their natural environment, marine biologists take sea voyages. When they reach their destination, perhaps near a coral reef or other habitat, the scientists dive into the water to collect samples.

Because of the cold temperatures below the surface of the sea, marine biologists must wear wetsuits to keep warm. They use scuba gear to help them breathe under water. They may carry a tool, called a *slurp gun,* which can suck a fish into a specimen bag without hurting it. While underwater, biologists must be on the lookout for dangerous fish. They take great care not to damage the marine environment.

Octopus Fun Facts
- The largest octopus is the North Pacific Octopus (*Octopus dofleini*). It can grow to over 30 feet and weighs more than 100 pounds.
- The smallest octopus is the Californian Octopus (*Octopus micropyrsus*). It is only 3/8 inch to 1 inch in length.
- When threatened, octopuses often try to escape by releasing a cloud of purple-black ink to confuse the enemy.

Shark Fun Facts
- Slow growing sharks, such as the tope shark and piked dogfish, can live more than 40 years.
- Only 32 species of sharks have ever attacked people.
- There are more than 350 species of sharks.
- Sharks eat almost anything, including fishes, crustaceans, mollusks, marine mammals, and other sharks.

Marine biologists measuring a loggerhead turtle (Jeff Rotman Photography/Photo Researchers, Inc.)

Marine biologists also gather specimens from tidal pools along the shore. They may collect samples at the same time of day for days at a time. They keep samples from different pools separate and carefully write down the pool's location, the types of specimens taken, and their measurements. It is important to keep accurate records.

After they collect specimens, scientists keep them in a special portable aquarium tank on the ship. After returning to land, sometimes weeks

What Aquarists Do

Aquarists are responsible for the maintenance of aquatic exhibits. Aquarists work in aquariums, oceanariums, and marine research facilities. Their work is critical because it keeps the fish and other sea life in these exhibits healthy and thriving. Different kinds of fish require very specific temperatures, chemical levels, and food in their tanks in order to survive. Aquarists maintain these conditions and keep very detailed records of the health and behavior of the fish, noting any problems or changes to the conditions of the tank.

Aquarists must have strong science and math skills in order to keep up with their technical work. Almost all institutions require aquarists to have a bachelor's degree in a biological science. Because aquarists help collect new specimens in the field and must sometimes enter large tanks, they must be in good physical condition and be certified to dive. With increased experience and education, an aquarist may eventually become more involved with research and be promoted to a higher professional position such as curator. Aquarists earn an average salary of $27,000 a year, and the outlook for this profession remains strong.

For more information on becoming an aquarist, contact the American Zoo and Aquarium Association, http://www.aza.org.

or months later, marine biologists study the specimens in a laboratory. They might check the amount of oxygen in a sea turtle's bloodstream to learn how the turtle can stay underwater for so long. Or they might measure the blood chemistry of an arctic fish to discover how it can survive frigid temperatures.

Marine biologists study changing conditions of the ocean, such as temperature or chemicals that have polluted the water. They try to see how those changes affect the plants and animals that live there. If certain species become extinct or are no longer safe to eat, the world's food supply grows smaller. Through underwater exploration, these scientists have discovered that humans are destroying the world's coral reefs. They have also charted the migration of whales and counted the decreasing numbers of certain species. They have seen dolphins being caught by accident in tuna fishermen's nets. By telling people their discoveries through written reports and research papers, marine biologists sometimes make important worldwide changes.

EXPLORING

- Visit your local aquarium to learn about marine life and about the life of a marine biologist.
- If you live near an ocean you can collect shells and other specimens. Keep a notebook to record details about what you find and where.
- You can begin diving training while in high school. Between the ages of 12 and 15 you can earn a Junior Open Water Diver certification. This allows you to dive in the company of a certified adult. When you turn 15 you can upgrade your certification to Open Water Diver.
- Take up hobbies, such as swimming, boating, snorkeling, or fishing.
- Turtles and fish make good pets for future marine biologists.

Education and Training

If you want to be a marine biologist, you should like math, science, and computers, as all are critical in this career. Biology, botany, and chemistry classes are important to take in high school. You also should be able to ask questions and solve problems, observe small details carefully, do research, and work out mathematical problems. A bachelor's degree is a bare minimum for this career, but most marine biologists have a master's degree or a doctorate (Ph.D.).

Earnings

Salaries vary depending on how much education and experience you have. The average biologist with a master's degree earns about $49,000 yearly. Those who have doctorates in marine biology can earn as much as $80,000 a year. Senior scientists or full professors at universities can earn more than $100,000 a year.

Outlook

There is a lot of competition for the best jobs in marine biology. Opportunities in research are especially hard to find. If you have an advanced degree and specialized knowledge in mathematics and computer science you will have the best chances for employment. Changes in the Earth's environment, such as global warming, will most likely require more research and so create more jobs. Marine biologists should be able to find jobs managing the world's fisheries, making medicines from marine organisms, and cultivating marine food alternatives, such as seaweed and plankton.

FOR MORE INFO

For information on careers, contact
American Society of Limnology and Oceanography
5400 Bosque Boulevard, Suite 680
Waco, TX 76710
Tel: 800-929-2756
http://www.aslo.org

For links to marine labs, summer intern and course opportunities, and links to career information, visit this website.
Marine Biology Web Page, State University of New York
http://life.bio.sunysb.edu/marinebio/mbweb.html

For information on diving instruction and certification, contact
Professional Association of Diving Instructors
30151 Tomas Street
Rancho Santa Margarita, CA 92688
Tel: 800-729-7234
http://www.padi.com

Meteorologists

What Meteorologists Do

Meteorologists study weather conditions to forecast changes in the weather. They gather information daily, and sometimes hourly, from weather satellites above the earth. They use this information about the atmosphere to make charts and maps that show regional and local temperatures, rainfall, winds, pressure areas, and cloud coverage.

Most meteorologists specialize in one specific area. The largest group of specialists is called *weather forecasters*. Many of them work at radio and television studios. They forecast short- and long-range weather during news shows.

To make their predictions, weather forecasters get weather information from many sources. In addition to weather satellites and weather radar, information is also sent from remote sensors and observers in many parts of the world. Meteorologists use advanced computer models of the world's atmosphere to help with their long-range, short-range, and local-area forecasts.

Some meteorologists, called *climatologists*, study past weather conditions of a region over a long period of time. They try to predict future weather patterns for the region.

Weather Fun Facts

- An average-sized cloud droplet is 0.012 millimeters in diameter. A large raindrop is around 6 millimeters in diameter.
- The largest hailstone on record in the United States was 7.5 inches in diameter and weighed 1.67 pounds. It fell in Coffeyville, Kansas, on September 3, 1970.
- Dirty snow melts faster than clean snow.
- The largest snowflake on record was 8 inches wide.
- You can tell the temperature in degrees Fahrenheit by counting the number of clicks a cricket makes in 15 seconds and then adding 37.

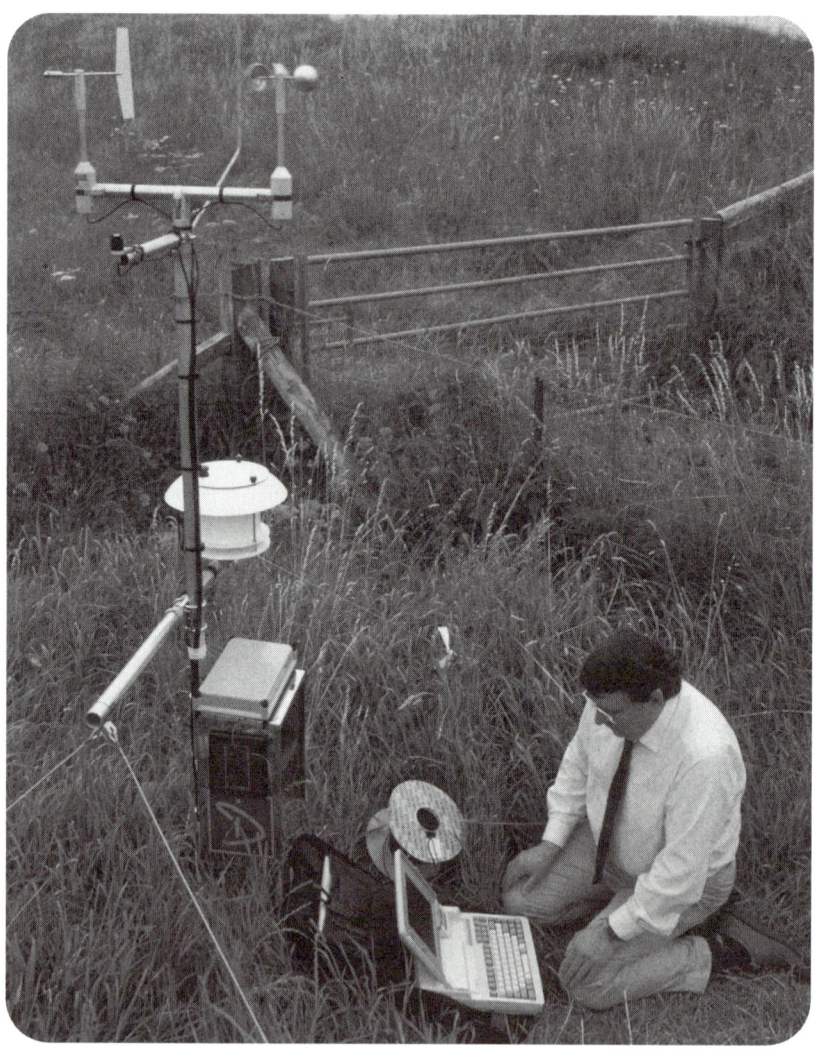

A meteorologist downloads weather data from a monitoring station. (David Parker / Photo Researchers, Inc.)

Other meteorologists study only air currents, pollution, radiation, or hurricanes. Some do not forecast at all. They teach in colleges and universities.

The lives and work of many people depend on how meteorologists report weather information. Airline pilots, ship captains, farmers, and everyday people all rely on the careful and detailed work of meteorologists.

Education and Training

If you are interested in meteorology, you should like science, especially physics and chemistry. In high school, you should take as many classes as you can in physical sciences. Mechanical drawing is another good class to take.

All meteorologists need at least a bachelor's degree. Many of the best jobs, though, require a master's degree or a doctorate (Ph.D.). The best research jobs and nearly all teaching jobs in colleges and universities go to meteorologists who have advanced graduate training.

EXPLORING

The Weather Channel website at http://www.weather.com has information on travel, weather, and health (such as allergies). Also check out these weather websites:

- Accuu/Weather Inc., http://www.accuweather.com
- The National Weather Service, http://www.nws.noaa.gov
- Weather Wiz Kids, http://www.weatherwizkids.com

Weather Folklore

People have tried to predict and control the weather since the beginning of time. Here are some common weather sayings, some silly, some based on scientific theory.

- If animals grow an especially thick coat of fur, expect a cold winter.
- The calendar day of the month when the first snowflake falls will signal the number of snowfalls for that winter.
- If you hear an owl hoot in the daytime, a storm is coming.
- When clouds look like chicken scratches it will soon rain.
- The weather on the 12 days between Christmas and January 5 foretells the weather for each of the next 12 months.
- "When the wind is in the south, the rain is in its mouth."
- A cold and wet June spoils the rest of the year.

FOR MORE INFO

The following organization offers a newsletter, journals, employment announcements, scholarships, and student information:

American Meteorological Society
45 Beacon Street
Boston, MA 02108
Tel: 617-227-2425
http://www.ametsoc.org

This government agency describes and predicts changes in the environment. It also manages marine and coastal resources.

National Oceanographic and Atmospheric Administration
U.S. Department of Commerce
14th Street and Constitution Ave., NW,
Room 6217
Washington, DC 20230
Tel: 202-482-6090
http://www.noaa.gov

For job announcements, a newsletter, and science links, contact

National Weather Association
1697 Capri Way
Charlottesville, VA 22911
Tel: 434-296-9966
http://www.nwas.org

Earnings

Salaries in the meteorology field vary widely. Beginning meteorologists with a bachelor's degree who work for the federal government make starting salaries of $24,000–$30,000 a year. Those with a master's degree start at $30,000–$36,000, and those with Ph.D.'s earn starting salaries between $47,000 and $60,000 a year. Broadcast meteorologists can earn between $20,000 and $100,000 or more depending on where they work.

Outlook

The meteorology field is expected to grow at an average rate during the next 10 years. The National Weather Service employs the highest number of meteorologists, but new jobs will be most plentiful in private industry. Companies that offer detailed weather information to specific groups, such as farmers, construction firms, and investors, will offer many new positions for qualified candidates.

Oceanographers

What Oceanographers Do

Oceanographers study the oceans. They perform experiments and gather information about the water, plant and animal life, and the ocean floor. They study the motion of waves, currents, and tides. They also look at water temperature, the chemical makeup of the ocean water, oil deposits on the ocean floor, and pollution levels at different depths of the oceans.

Oceanographers use several inventions specially designed for long- and short-term underwater observation. They use deep-sea equipment, such as submarines and observation tanks. Underwater devices called bathyspheres enable an oceanographer to stay underwater for several hours or even days. For short observations or to explore areas such as underwater caves, these scientists use deep-sea and scuba diving gear that straps onto the body to supply them with oxygen.

Oceanographers do most of their work out of the water. While at sea, they gather the scientific information that they need. Then they spend months or years in offices, laboratories, or libraries examining the data. Oceanographers use information

Did You Know?
- Oceans cover nearly three-quarters of the planet's surface.
- Ocean depth averages 2.3 miles.
- The ocean's food webs support more life than any other ecosystem.
- The oceans have vast stores of valuable minerals, including nickel, iron, manganese, copper, and cobalt.
- The surface temperature of Earth's oceans ranges from about 86°F at the equator to about 29°F near the poles. The world's warmest water is in the Persian Gulf, where surface temperatures reach 96°F.

such as water temperature changes between the surface and the lower depths to predict droughts and monsoon rains.

Most oceanographers specialize in one of four areas. Those who study ocean plants and animals are called *biological oceanographers* or *marine biologists*. They collect information on the behavior, needs, and activities of the wildlife in a specific area of the ocean water. Whale specialists may have a marine biology background.

Physical oceanographers study ocean temperature and the atmosphere above the water. They study the greenhouse effect, or the warming of the planet's surface. They observe the melting of the ice on the Arctic and Antarctic Circles. They calculate the movement of the warm water through the oceans to help meteorologists predict weather patterns. *Geological oceanographers* study the ocean floor. They use instruments that monitor the ocean floor and the minerals found there from a far distance. In areas where the ocean is too deep for any man-made equipment to go, they use remote sensors. *Geochemical oceanographers* study the chemical makeup of ocean water and the ocean floor. They detect oil well sites. They study pollution problems and possible chemical causes for plant and animal diseases in a particular region of the water. *Geochemical oceanographers* are called in after oil spills to check the level of damage to the water.

EXPLORING

- If you live near coastal regions, you can easily become familiar with oceans and ocean life through trips to the water. Read all you can about rocks, minerals, or aquatic life. If you live or travel near an oceanography research center or an aquarium, spend some time studying their exhibits, and ask lots of questions.
- If you do not live near water, try to find summer camps or programs that make trips to coastal areas. Learn all you can about the geology, atmosphere, and plant and animal life of the area where you live, regardless of whether water is present.

Oceans of the World

Name	Square Miles	Greatest Depth (in feet)
Pacific	64,186,300	35,810
Atlantic	33,420,000	28,232
Indian	28,350,500	25,344
Arctic	5,105,700	18,399

The area figures for the oceans include all adjoining seas, so that all the continuous saltwater (the world ocean) is included. For example, the Mediterranean and Black seas are included in the Atlantic Ocean. The Bering and China seas are included in the Pacific Ocean. The Arabian Sea is included in the Indian Ocean.

Education and Training

To become an oceanographer, you will need at least a bachelor's degree in chemistry, biology, geology, or physics. For most research or teaching positions, you will need a master's degree or doctorate (Ph.D.) in oceanography.

Earnings

Entry-level salaries in oceanography for those with bachelor's degrees average about $26,700 a year. A mid-range salary for experienced oceanographers with advanced degrees is around $67,000. The highest paid oceanographers can make more than $100,000 a year.

Outlook

Jobs for oceanographers should grow at an average rate over the next 10 years. The growing interest in understanding and protecting the environment will help to create new jobs, as will careers related to fisheries. Pharmaceutical and biotechnology companies will need oceanographers as they look to extract resources from the sea to make new drugs and other products. Candidates with advanced degrees will have the best chances of getting jobs.

FOR MORE INFO

For information on oceanography and marine science careers, contact the following organizations:

American Society of Limnology and Oceanography
5400 Bosque Boulevard, Suite 680
Waco, TX 76710
Tel: 800-929-2756
http://www.aslo.org

Marine Technology Society
5565 Sterrett Place, Suite 108
Columbia, MD 21044
Tel: 410-884-5330
http://www.mtsociety.org

The Oceanography Society
PO Box 1931
Rockville, MD 20849
Tel: 301-251-7708
http://www.tos.org

Paleontologists

What Paleontologists Do

Paleontologists examine rocks and fossils. Fossils are the remains or traces of prehistoric plants and animals that were preserved in the rocks of the earth.

Paleontologists study rock formations to learn more about the history of life on Earth, the placement of land and water, and the location of important substances, such as oil, gas, and coal. Rocks give clues about ancient environments and climates.

Fossils help paleontologists figure out the age of rocks. Once the age of the fossil is determined, then scientists can estimate the age of the surrounding rock. Paleontologists also study fossils to figure out the age of a particular type of plant or animal. They determine when it lived and compare it to similar plants and animals from various time periods. This helps them trace the animal or plant's evolution to see how it has changed or adapted from one time period to the next.

Man or Medicine?

In the 19th century, some Chinese pharmacists made regular trips to a limestone hill near Beijing to dig for fossils. They went not for research, but to collect the fossils for grinding into medicine. The bones they collected were later recognized as near-human, dating from about a half-million years before. In 1929, part of a skull was discovered in the same location, as well as a new species, Peking Man, a species that preceded *Homo sapiens* (modern man and woman) in the evolutionary chain.

Paleontologists spend a lot of time in laboratories. They also travel throughout the world to work in the field—sometimes for months at a time—collecting specimens to examine. Fieldwork is sometimes painstaking. It takes patience and dedication to gather and interpret detailed information about the earth. Paleontologists use dynamite and jackhammers, masonry hammers, chisels, putty knives, trowels, sifters, and soft-bristled paintbrushes. They always carry a notebook and pen or pencil to make detailed notes.

Education and Training

Paleontology is a subspecialty in the field of geology. Paleontologists usually study geology in college, although some major in fields such as botany or zoology. After earning a bachelor's degree, students go on to study paleontology in graduate school.

Most paleontologists earn a doctorate (Ph.D.). Those with master's degrees may be able to find work as technicians, either as preparators, collections managers, or lab supervisors. Those who wish to do research, exploration, college-level teaching, or museum work will need a doctorate.

Paleontologists usually work on teams with other scientists, so it is important to develop good communication skills. You will also need good computer skills to handle large amounts of data.

EXPLORING

- Check with a local museum about field trips open to the public. The museum may also be able to direct you to local rock- or fossil-collecting clubs.
- Contact your state geological society for information about fossils in your area and fossil-hunting opportunities.
- The Midwest and Great Plains states are especially rich in fossil beds. This is because an inland sea once covered these areas. Sediments from this sea protected the skeletons of creatures and kept them from being moved about.
- Professional geology societies publish brochures on fossil hunting and the kinds of fossils available in different areas. See the end of this article for contact information.

Earnings

Paleontologists with bachelor's degrees who work in technician positions earn about $42,000 a year. Those with doctorates earn an average of $79,000 a year.

Outlook

There are few job openings for paleontologists, so the competition is stiff. More paleontologists graduate every year than there are positions open for them. There are also fewer educational opportunities, as schools close geology departments in order to cut costs. Paleontologists who have

These paleontologists are excavating the skeleton of the dinosaur Albertasaurus in Alberta, Canada. (Richard T. Nowitz / Photo Researchers, Inc.)

Fossil Hunting Tips

- Quarries, roadcuts, and cliffs are good places to find fossils. Always remember to put safety first. You may also need special permission to explore some areas, so check with your parents, teachers, or another authority before starting your search.
- Many state geological offices sell maps and books on the state's geology, including paleontology. Check with the U.S. Geological Survey or your public library for publications and reports on the paleontology of your area. Also try the bookstore of a natural history museum.
- There may be an amateur paleontology organization in your area. It may publish information or sponsor fossil-hunting expeditions.
- There are rules and laws for fossil-hunting in your area. It is up to you to find out what they are. Usually you need permission from the owner to collect on private land. You need a permit to collect in national parks and land managed by the Bureau of Land Management. Remember not to deface sites, litter, or put yourself or others in any danger.

published research and who cross-specialize in fields such as zoology or botany will be the best candidates for jobs.

FOR MORE INFO

For a brochure on careers in the geological sciences, as well as information about scholarships and internships, contact
American Geological Institute
4220 King Street
Alexandria, VA 22302
Tel: 703-379-2480
http://www.agiweb.org

The Geological Society of America
PO Box 9140
Boulder, CO 80301
Tel: 888-443-4472
http://www.geosociety.org

For a listing of amateur paleontology groups across the United States, visit
The Society for Amateur Scientists
http://www.sas.org/AmateurGroups/PaleontologyAmateur.html

Petrologists

What Petrologists Do

Petrologists are closely related to geologists. Geologists study the overall formation of the earth and the movements of the earth's crust. Petrologists focus on rocks and rock formations. They study the origin and history of rocks and rock formations and investigate the composition (physical makeup) of rocks. They study a wide variety of substances ranging from diamonds and gold to petroleum deposits that may be buried deep beneath the earth's surface.

Much of the science of petrology relates to removing minerals, petroleum, gold, and other natural resources from rock formations within the earth. Petrologists often work for mining companies. For example, they may work as part of an oil drilling team and help discover whether certain rock formations are likely to contain oil. They might also work on a mining operation searching for gold and analyzing rock samples to see whether they contain any of this precious metal. Petrologists work alongside *hydrologists* (who study earth's water systems), *mineralogists* (who examine and classify minerals), and other scientists.

A Quick Rock Wrap-Up

There are three major classes of rocks: igneous, sedimentary, and metamorphic.

- Igneous rocks are formed by the cooling of molten mixtures of minerals, called magmas, which are found far below the earth's crust.
- Sedimentary rocks are formed of loose materials, such as mud, sand, pebbles, and bits of organic matter. These materials are called sediment. After millions of years, layers of sediment solidify into rock because of chemical action and the pressure caused by overlying layers of material.
- Metamorphic rocks are formed underground by the alteration of sedimentary or igneous rocks. This alteration can be caused by heat, pressure, chemical action, or movement of the earth's crust.

Petrologists spend time in the field gathering samples and in the laboratory studying those samples. They use rock samples, photographs, and diagrams to describe the rock formations they are studying. They use chemicals to break down rocks and rock materials to uncover certain elements within the rocks. They use X rays and other tools to look at and test the samples so that they can draw conclusions from their analysis.

Once petrologists complete an analysis of the rock formations, they prepare a written report of their findings. These reports are usually sent to managers at a drill site but they may also be used for other research purposes. These reports often are used to determine whether a mining operation should continue. Petrologists also may write reports for the government.

EXPLORING

- Participate in your school's science club, and ask your science teacher about the field of petrology.
- Visit a natural history museum and see if you can arrange an interview with a geologist or petrologist who may be on staff.
- Check out some of the following books:

  Hooper, Meredith. *The Pebble in My Pocket: A History of Our Earth.* New York: Viking, 1996.

  Perrault, Chris. *The Best Book of Fossils, Rocks, and Minerals.* Larousse Kingfisher Chambers, 2000.

  Symes, R. F. *Eyewitness: Rocks and Minerals.* New York: DK Publishing, 2000.

Education and Training

Petrologists must have a college education. The best way to become a petrologist is to earn a master's degree or doctorate (Ph.D.). It is possible to find a position with a bachelor's degree but an advanced degree is often required, especially if you want to advance in the field. Many students begin by majoring in geology or paleontology (the study of fossils) in college. They

> ## What Petroleum Technicians Do
>
> *Petroleum technicians* help explore, drill for, and produce petroleum. There are many different kinds of petroleum technicians. Some help geologists and earth scientists scientifically predict and locate where oil can be found. Others help engineers develop better drilling machinery to bring oil from underground or from deep beneath the sea. Others help engineers develop better storage and pipeline systems to distribute oil. Some technicians do the actual drilling. Others monitor wells once they start producing oil. Technicians also maintain equipment and machinery.
>
> Technicians may work in a laboratory, an office, or, most likely, on a drilling rig either onshore or offshore. Drilling rig technicians work in all-weather activities and put in long, irregular hours. Some petroleum technicians have to handle heavy off-the-road machinery and other sophisticated scientific instruments.
>
> To become a petroleum technician, you must be at least a high school graduate. For certain jobs, you will need a two-year petroleum technology degree from a technical or community college. Only a few jobs require a four-year college degree. Beginning salaries start at about $21,000 a year. Technicians with more experience can make more than $50,000 a year. The employment outlook for petroleum technicians is generally good, with more jobs going to workers with specialized skills and ample experience.

begin training in petrology when they enter graduate school. You need a solid background in geology, chemistry, and mathematics.

Earnings

The average salary for petrologists with a bachelor's degree is about $36,000 a year. With a master's degree or doctorate, petrologists earn a mid-level salary of about $67,000 a year. Top-level petrologists employed in private industry can earn more than $100,000 a year.

Outlook

Jobs for petrologists should grow at an average rate in coming years. As a result of a worldwide increase in fuel prices, oil companies are looking for new oil sites around the world. If this trend continues, there will be a steady demand for petrologists with advanced degrees. New environmental regulations will also create jobs for petrologists in environmental protection and reclamation work.

FOR MORE INFO

For information on geology careers, contact

American Association of Petroleum Geologists
Communications Department
PO Box 979
Tulsa, OK 74101
Tel: 800-364-2274
http://www.aapg.org

American Geological Institute
4220 King Street
Alexandria, VA 22302
Tel: 703-379-2480
http://www.agiweb.org

For career information and job listings, contact

The Geological Society of America
PO Box 9140
Boulder, CO 80301
Tel: 888-443-4472
http://www.geosociety.org

Pharmacologists

What Pharmacologists Do

Pharmacologists are scientists who study how drugs, chemicals, and other materials affect human beings and animals. Some pharmacologists develop and test new drugs for doctors to use in treating disease. Others test chemicals, pollutants, and other materials found in homes, farms, and factories to see how they affect animals and humans.

Pharmacologists in drug research study the effects of medical substances on the human body. Their goal is to discover the good effects and the possibly harmful side effects that a drug may have. Using this information, pharmacologists can tell drug companies the best way to manufacture the drug. They tell physicians when and how the drug should be given to patients.

Pharmacologists who specialize in testing chemicals, pollutants, and other substances in the environment and in food look for possible harmful effects. They do research on industrial materials, pesticides, food preservatives and colorings, and even on common household items such as paints, aerosol sprays, and cleaning fluids, to find out whether they are safe to use.

Pharmacologists do most of their research in laboratories using laboratory animals, plants, and tissue samples from animals and human donors. *Clinical pharmacologists* test drugs on human subjects. Some pharmacologists

Aspirin and Its Many Uses

Pharmacologists try to find new therapies and treatments. They also discover new uses for drugs that have been around for a long time. Aspirin was introduced as a painkiller more than 100 years ago. Now, as a result of pharmacologists' research, it is used as an effective treatment for strokes, heart attacks, and arthritis.

specialize in particular parts of the body. For example, *neuropharmacologists* study drugs that affect the nervous system. *Cardiovascular pharmacologists* study drugs for the heart, lungs, and circulatory systems. *Behavioral pharmacologists* specialize in the effects of drugs on mood and behavior.

Education and Training

To be a pharmacologist, you must have a good background in science and mathematics. In high school and college, you should take as many courses as possible in basic science, chemistry, biology, organic chemistry, and mathematics. Sharpen your writing skills in English courses, as pharmacologists write many research reports.

Nearly all pharmacologists must have a doctorate (Ph.D.). Earning a doctorate in pharmacology requires

EXPLORING

- Look for these books in your library or bookstore:
  Foster, Steven. *101 Medicinal Herbs: An Illustrated Guide.* Interweave Press, 1998.
  Janos, Elisabeth. *Country Folk Medicine: Tales of Skunk Oil, Sassafras Tea, and Other Old-Time Remedies.* Budget Book Service, 1995.
- When you are in a drugstore with an adult, take a look at the directions, warnings, and effects of various over the counter medications, such as cold medicine or antacids. Also, ask the pharmacist for information about a career in this field.

Can You Say Pharmacopoeia?

A pharmacopoeia is an official list of drugs that are considered of proven medical value. Pharmacopoeias describe drugs, give ways to test their purity and strength, tell how to prepare them, and list average doses. They are authorized by governments to provide high, uniform standards for drugs. Most countries have national pharmacopoeias. The *United States Pharmacopoeia* (U.S.P.) is the standard for the enforcement of federal drug laws. It was first published in 1820 and is revised every five years.

> ### Gardening for a Cure
>
> Before modern medicine and prescription drugs were invented, people used plants to cure illnesses. Malaria was first treated effectively by Peruvian Indians who used the extract of cinchona tree bark to help people with the fever. For most of the 20th century, however, doctors and drug developers have ignored the success of ethnobotany (the practice of deriving medicine from plants). Less than 10 percent of the 450,000–750,000 existing plant species have been studied for their medicinal properties. But this is changing. Some of today's biggest drug companies, including Eli Lilly, Glaxo, and Merck, see a future in ethnobotany and are researching and developing medicines from plants. Recent ethnobotanical research has led to discoveries that could be used to treat AIDS, respiratory infections, and other illnesses.

four to five years of study after college, usually at a medical school or pharmacy school. Because pharmacology is so closely related to the practice of medicine, many pharmacologists are also medical doctors (M.D.'s) or veterinarians (D.V.M.'s).

Earnings

Pharmacologists earn yearly salaries ranging from $32,000 (for those with bachelor's degrees) to well over $110,000 (for those with Ph.D.'s). The national average salary for medical scientists, a group that includes pharmacologists, is $67,000. Pharmacologists with the highest salaries are either those who supervise teams of people in large laboratories or senior faculty in colleges and universities.

Outlook

There will be a great demand for health care services and products in the coming years, especially as the elderly population grows. There will be plenty of jobs for pharmacologists, especially for those who develop new drugs. They will play an important part in fighting diseases such as AIDS and cancer.

FOR MORE INFO

For information about careers and educational opportunities for students, contact

American Society for Clinical Pharmacology and Therapeutics
528 North Washington Street
Alexandria, VA 22314
Tel: 703-836-6981
http://www.ascpt.org

For information about student chapters, news releases, and publications, contact

American Association of Pharmaceutical Sciences
2107 Wilson Boulevard, Suite 700
Arlington, VA 22201
Tel: 703-243-9650
http://www.aaps.org

Physicists

What Physicists Do

Physics is a science dealing with the interaction of matter (solids, liquids, and gases) and energy. *Physicists* study the behavior and structure of matter, the ways that energy is generated and transferred, and the relationships between matter and energy. Some physicists teach in high schools and colleges, some work for the federal government, and some work for industrial laboratories. Wherever they work, physicists spend a great deal of time doing research, performing laboratory experiments, and studying the results.

Theoretical physicists try to understand how matter and energy work. For example, they may study electrical or nuclear energy, try to define the laws of each, and then write them up in mathematical formulas. *Experimental physicists* perform experiments that test exactly what various kinds of matter and energy do. They then try to come up with practical ways to use them. For example, they may work in the communications industries, such as television, telephone, or radio, to invent technologies for better pictures or better sound.

Physicists Tie Themselves in Knots

Theoretical physicists Thomas Fink and Yong Mao of the Cavendish Laboratory in Cambridge, England, came up with six new ways to tie a knot in a neck tie. They used analytical techniques to break down tie-knotting steps into a set of mathematical formulas. They found that there are 85 ways to tie a tie, but only 10 are any good. They range from a simple four-move knot to a complicated 10-move nightmare.

Physicists work in many areas. Some study atoms to learn the secrets of nuclear energy. Others work with engineers to find the best ways to build bridges and dams. Others conduct experiments for petroleum companies to find better ways to obtain, refine, and use crude oil. Physicists are important in the space program. They try to figure out what outer space is actually like, and they design and test spaceships. Physicists often work with other scientists, such as chemists, biologists, and geologists. Biophysics and geophysics are two fields of science that were created when these scientists began to work together.

Physicists may specialize in mechanics, heat, optics (light), acoustics (sound), electricity and magnetism, electronics, particle physics (atoms and molecules), nuclear physics, or physics of fluids. All physicists must have keen powers of observation and a strong curiosity about the world around them.

Education and Training

Physicists who have only a bachelor's degree from a four-year college can qualify for basic research and technician jobs. Those with teaching certificates can work in secondary school. However, most physicists must further their education in order to advance in the field. The more challenging and rewarding jobs go to physicists who have master's degrees and doctorates (Ph.D.'s). Many of the most able physicists go on to complete postdoctoral education.

EXPLORING

- Ask your science teachers to assign some physics experiments.
- Join a science club or start one at your school.
- Enter a project in a science fair. If your school does not sponsor science fairs, you may find fairs sponsored by your school district, state, or a science society.

Earnings

The national average salary for physicists is $87,500. Physicists with bach-

The World's Most Famous Scientist

Have you ever looked at the night sky and wondered when the universe began, if it is growing, or how to track the passing of time in outer space? Stephen Hawking has, and he has spent the better part of his life providing possible answers to these and many more questions about our universe. Stephen is a *cosmologist*, a physicist who studies the origins and structure of space and time and their relationship to the earth and everything beyond it. From a very early age, Stephen showed a natural talent for math and science. When he was 16, he and his friends even built a computer out of spare clock parts and a switchboard.

Stephen's curiosity about the universe and physics continued throughout his education at England's Oxford and Cambridge Universities. He quickly made a name for himself, both for his innovative theories and likeable personality. When he was in college, Stephen was diagnosed with a disease called ALS, also known as Lou Gehrig's disease. Because of his disease, Stephen is confined to a wheelchair and must speak through the use of a computer program. But he has never let his ALS slow him down. In fact, Stephen has become the world's most famous scientist. His books on black holes and the origins of the universe have become international best-sellers. He has traveled around the world, met with many famous leaders, and has appeared in both film and television.

To learn more about Stephen Hawking, cosmology, and physics in general, visit his website at http://www.hawking.org.uk, and look for the book *Stephen Hawking: Physicist and Educator* (Facts On File, 2005) in your school or local library.

elor's degrees working as technicians in aerospace earn average salaries of $53,000 a year. The highest paid physicists have doctorates and many years of experience.

Outlook

Employment prospects for physicists over the next decade are favorable. Increased government research, especially in the Departments of Defense, Energy, and Commerce, will create new positions. There should also be steady job growth for physicists in industry, research development laboratories, and colleges and universities. The best jobs will go to those with doctoral degrees.

FOR MORE INFO

For employment statistics and information on jobs and career planning, contact
American Institute of Physics
Division of Careers Placement
One Physics Ellipse
College Park, MD 20740
Tel: 301-209-3100
http://www.aip.org

For employment information, contact
Canadian Association of Physicists
Suite 112, MacDonald Building
150 Louis Pasteur Priv.
Ottawa, ON Canada K1N 6N5
Tel: 613-562-5614
http://www.cap.ca

Fermilab offers internships, employment opportunities, and general information. Friends of Fermilab is a nonprofit organization that supports precollege education programs.
Fermilab
PO Box 500
Batavia, IL 60510
Tel: 630-840-3000
http://www.fnal.gov

Soil Scientists

What Soil Scientists Do

Soil is one of our most important natural resources. It provides the nutrients necessary to grow food for hundreds of millions of people. To use soil wisely and keep it from washing away or being damaged, *soil scientists* analyze it and find the best ways to manage it. Soil scientists collect soil samples and study their chemical and physical characteristics. They study how soil responds to fertilizer and other farming practices. This helps farmers decide what types of crops to grow on certain soils.

Soil scientists do much of their work outdoors. They go to fields to take soil samples. They spend many hours meeting with farmers and discussing ways to avoid soil damage. They may suggest that a farmer grow crops on different parts of a farm every few years so that the unused soil can recover. Soil scientists may also recommend that a farmer use various fertilizers to put nutrients back into the soil. They may

Dirty Artwork

The appeal of soil study is not always scientific; sometimes the beauty of the soil inspires scientists. Hungarian soil scientist Erika Micheli discovered a collection of wavy, multicolored soil layers after a surface mining operation left the ground exposed. The rippled formations were made by the burrowing of prehistoric groundhogs, erosion, and pressure from frozen rainwater. Micheli's study of the formations led to cautions to area farmers about the way they use fertilizers and pesticides. The formations also inspired Micheli to create works of art in the form of lacquered, 3-D portraits of the soil.

What Soil Conservation Technicians Do

Soil conservation technicians help people develop plans to use soil wisely. They assist soil scientists as they show farmers how to rotate crops so that the nutrients in the soil are not used up. They also help foresters with growing and harvesting plans so that trees are not cut down before they mature.

Soil conservation technicians help engineers survey land. They plan drainage systems and irrigation systems. Soil conservation technicians make maps from aerial photographs. They inspect specific areas to determine what conservation methods are needed.

Soil conservation technicians called *cartographic technicians* chart or map areas of the earth. *Geodetic technicians* help collect and analyze information about the size, shape, and gravity of the earth. *Meteorological technicians* analyze or predict weather and its effect on the earth's surface. *Surveying technicians* gather information for the design of highways and dams or for making topographic maps. *Range conservationists* plan range conservation programs that help people who raise livestock operate their ranges better.

To be a soil conservation technician you should enroll in a technical institute or a junior or community college where you will earn an associate's degree in soil conservation. Technicians make an average salary of $33,000 a year. Salaries in private industry are usually lower than those in government jobs. Job growth for soil conservation technicians is expected to be somewhat slow over the next several years, as government spending for research will be lower. However, technicians can also find employment in private industry.

suggest ways to cover crops to keep the wind from blowing the soil away.

Soil scientists work for agricultural research laboratories, crop production companies, and other organizations. They also work with road departments to advise them about the quality and condition of the soil over which roads will be built.

Some soil scientists travel to foreign countries to conduct research and observe the way other scientists treat the soil. Many also teach at colleges, universities, and agricultural schools.

Education and Training

To become a soil scientist, you need a solid background in mathematics and science, especially the physical and earth sciences. You should also be curious, be able to solve complex problems, and have good writing and speaking skills.

The best way to become a soil scientist is to go to college and earn a bachelor's degree in agricultural or soil science. Then you should go on to earn a master's degree in agricultural science. A degree in biology, physics, or chemistry might also be sufficient, but you should take some courses in agriculture. With a bachelor's degree in agricultural science, you can get some nonresearch jobs, but you will not be able to advance very far. Most research and teaching positions require a doctorate (Ph.D.).

EXPLORING

- If you live in an agricultural community, you might be able to find some opportunities for part-time or summer work on a farm or ranch.
- Join a Future Farmers of America (FFA) program to learn about farming and agricultural research.
- A local 4-H club can give you valuable experience in agriculture.
- Your county's soil conservation department may have educational programs and information about regional projects.

FOR MORE INFO

To learn about careers and issues that affect soil scientists, contact these organizations.

American Society of Agronomy/ Soil Science Society of America
677 South Segoe Road
Madison, WI 53711
Tel: 608-273-8080
http://www.soils.org

National Society of Consulting Soil Scientists
PMB 700, 325 Pennsylvania Avenue SE
Washington, DC 20003
Tel: 800-535-7148
http://www.nscss.org

A soil scientist conducts an erosion study. (Science Source / Photo Researchers, Inc.)

Earnings

Soil scientists earn an average yearly salary of $53,000. Those in entry-level positions may start at $30,000. The most experienced and educated workers can earn more than $80,000 a year.

Outlook

Agricultural problems will continue to be important in the coming years. However, job growth for soil scientists may be slow because of decreased government involvement in farming studies. Soil scientists should still be able to find work in private businesses, who will hire them for research and sales positions. There will also continue to be teaching positions available as current teachers change jobs or retire.

Zoologists

What Zoologists Do

Zoologists are biologists who study animals. They usually specialize in one animal group. *Entomologists* are experts on insects. *Ornithologists* study birds. *Mammalogists* focus on mammals. *Herpetologists* specialize in reptiles. *Ichthyologists* study fish. Some zoologists specialize even more and focus on a specific part or aspect of an animal. For example, a zoologist might study single-cell organisms, a particular variety of fish, or the behavior of one group of animals, such as elephants or bees.

Some zoologists are primarily teachers. Others spend most of their time doing research. Nearly all zoologists spend a major portion of their time at the computer. Most zoologists spend very little time outdoors (an average of two to eight weeks per year). In fact, junior scientists often spend more time in the field than senior scientists do. Senior scientists

Hope for the Manatees

Surveys show that there are no more than 700 West Indian manatees left in their habitat off the coast of Belize in Central America. There may be as few as 300. They have been killed or injured by boats or harmed by pollution from inland activities and deforestation. They have even been killed and marketed as fish (even though they are mammals).

A research program started by the Wildlife Preservation Trust International offers hope to the endangered manatee. The environmental air force called LightHawk charts the manatee's range and behavior. The data collected will be used to plan ways to save the manatee from extinction.

coordinate research, supervise other workers, and try to find funding. Raising money is an important activity for zoologists who work for government agencies or universities.

Basic research zoologists conduct experiments on live or dead animals in a laboratory or in natural surroundings. They make discoveries that might help humans. Such research in the past has led to discoveries about nutrition, aging, food production, and pest control. Some research zoologists work in the field with wild animals, such as whales. They trace their movements with radio transmitters and observe their eating habits, mating patterns, and other behavior. Researchers use all kinds of laboratory chemicals and equipment such as dissecting tools, microscopes, slides, electron microscopes, and other sophisticated machinery.

Zoologists in applied research use basic research to solve problems in medicine, conservation, and aquarium and zoo work. For example, applied researchers may develop a new drug for people or animals, a new pesticide, or a new type of pet food.

Many zoologists teach in colleges and universities while they do their own research. Some zoologists manage zoos and aquariums. Still others work for government agencies, private businesses, and research organizations.

Education and Training

Science classes, especially in biology, are important if you want to become a zoologist. You should also study English, communications, and computer science.

After high school, you must go to college to earn a bachelor's degree. A

EXPLORING

- Volunteer at your local zoo or aquarium.
- Ask your school librarian to help you find books and videos on animal behavior.
- Explore hobbies such as bird watching, insect collecting, or raising hamsters, rabbits, and other pets.
- Offer to pet sit for your neighbors. This will give you a chance to observe and care for animals.

What's in a Name?

What's in a name? A lot, if you consider the many terms zoologists use when referring to different animals.

Animal	Male	Female	Young
bear	boar	sow	cub
alligator	bull	cow	hatchling
horse	stallion	mare	foal, filly (female); colt (male)
ferrett	hob	jill	kit
gorilla	male	female	infant
duck	drake	duck	duckling
hawk	tiercel	hen	eyas
opossum	jack	jill	joey
tiger	tiger	tigress	cub

Source: *World Almanac for Kids* online, http://www.worldalmanacforkids.com

master's degree or doctorate (Ph.D.) is usually also required. You do not need to specialize your studies until you enter a master's degree program.

Earnings

Zoologists earn an average annual salary of $49,000 a year. Those with advanced degrees and who have established themselves in the field can make more than $80,000.

Outlook

There was rapid growth in the zoology field in the 1990s, but that has slowed somewhat. Competition for the highest paying research positions (those that require a Ph.D.) is very stiff.

There will be more positions available for zoologists with bachelor's or master's degrees. As opposed to many other science careers, zoologists will benefit from having a variety of experiences, as opposed to one specialization. This variety will make them eligible for a broader range of jobs.

FOR MORE INFO

For information about all areas of zoology contact

Society for Integrative and Comparative Biology
1313 Dolley Madison Blvd Suite 402
McLean, VA 22101
Tel: 800-955-1236
http://www.sicb.org

For information about zoological activities and organizations, schools, internships, and job opportunities, contact

American Institute of Biological Sciences
1444 I Street, NW, Suite 200
Washington, DC 20005
Tel: 202-628-1500
http://www.aibs.org

Glossary

accredited   approved as meeting established standards for providing good training and education; accreditation is usually given to a school or program by an independent organization of professionals

associate's degree   academic rank or title granted by a community or junior college or similar institution to graduates of a two-year program of education beyond high school

bachelor's degree   academic rank or title given to a person who has completed a four-year program of study at a college or university; also called an undergraduate degree or baccalaureate

certified   approved as meeting established requirements for skill, knowledge, and experience in a particular field; people are certified by the organization of professionals in their field

community college   public two-year college, attended by students who do not live at the college; graduates of a community college receive an associate's degree and may transfer to a four-year college or university to complete a bachelor's degree

diploma   certificate or document given by a school to show that a person has completed a course or has graduated from the school

doctorate   an academic rank or title (the highest) granted by a graduate school to a person who has completed a two- to three-year program after having received a master's degree; also known as doctor of philosophy, or Ph.D.

earth science   any of the sciences that deal with the Earth or its parts; geology, meteorology, and oceanography are earth sciences

graduate school school that people may attend after they have received their bachelor's degree; people who complete an educational program at a graduate school earn a master's degree or a doctorate

intern advanced student (usually one with at least some college training) in a professional field who is employed in a job that is intended to provide supervised practical experience for the student

internship 1. position or job of an intern (see **intern**); 2. period of time when a person is an intern

junior college a two-year college that offers courses like those in the first half of a four-year college program; graduates of a junior college usually receive an associate degree and may transfer to a four-year college or university to complete a bachelor's degree

liberal arts subjects covered by college courses that develop broad general knowledge rather than specific occupational skills; the liberal arts are often considered to include philosophy, literature and the arts, history, language, and some courses in the social sciences and natural sciences

licensed having formal permission from the proper authority to carry out an activity that would be illegal without that permission; for example, a person may be licensed to practice medicine or to drive a car

major (in college) academic field in which a student specializes and receives a degree

master's degree academic rank or title granted by a graduate school to a person who has completed a one- or two-year program after having received a bachelor's degree

natural sciences sciences that deal with matter, energy, and their interrelations and transformations; biology, chemistry, and physics are natural sciences

physical sciences sciences that deal with nonliving materials; astronomy, physics, and chemistry are physical sciences

private 1. not owned or controlled by the government (such as private industry or a private employment agency); 2. intended only for a particular person or group; not open to all (such as a private road or a private club)

public 1. provided or operated by the government (such as a public library); 2. open and available to everyone (such as a public meeting)

regulatory having to do with the rules and laws for carrying out an activity; regulatory agency, for example, is a government organization that sets up required procedures for how certain things should be done

scholarship gift of money to a student to help the student pay for further education

scientific method systematic manner of experimentation that all scientists use; consists of making an educated prediction, called a hypothesis, performing an experiment, observing and recording data, and then comparing results to the hypothesis, thereby proving or disproving it

social studies courses of study (such as civics, geography, and history) that deal with how human societies work

starting salary salary paid to a newly hired employee; the starting salary is usually a smaller amount than is paid to a more experienced worker

technical college private or public college offering two- or four-year programs in technical subjects; technical colleges offer courses in both general and technical subjects and award associate's degrees and bachelor's degrees

technician worker with specialized practical training in a mechanical or scientific subject who works under the supervision of scientists, engineers, or other professionals; technicians typically receive two years of college-level education after high school

technologist worker in a mechanical or scientific field with more training than a technician; technologists typically must have between two and four years of college-level education after high school

undergraduate student at a college or university who has not yet received a degree.

undergraduate degree see bachelor's degree

wage money that is paid in return for work done, especially money paid on the basis of the number of hours or days worked

Index of Job Titles

A
agricultural scientists 5–8
agronomists 5
analytical chemists 29
animal scientists 6–7
aquarists 50
archaeologists 9–12
astronomers 13–16
astrophysicists 13

B
behavioral pharmacologists 70
biochemists 17–20
biological oceanographers 58
biological scientists 21–24
biologists 21–24
botanists 21, 25–28

C
cardiovascular pharmacologists 70
cartographic technicians 78
celestial mechanics 13
chemists 29–32
climatologists 53
clinical geneticists 38
clinical pharmacologists 69
cosmologists 13

E
ecologists 26, 33–36
entomologists 81
ethnobotanists 26
experimental physicists 73

F
food chemists 29
forest ecologists 26, 33

G
genetic counselors 38
genetic engineers 38
geneticists 37–40
genetic scientists 37–40
geochemical oceanographers 58
geochemists 33
geodetic technicians 78
geological oceanographers 58
geological technicians 43
geologists 41–44
geophysicists 45–48

H
herpetologists 81
horticulturists 6
hydrogeologists 33
hydrologists 45, 65

I
ichthyologists 81

L
laboratory geneticists 37–38
life scientists 21–24

M
mammalogists 81
marine biologists 49–52, 58
marine geologists 41

meteorological technicians 78
meteorologists 45, 53–56
microbiologists 23
mineralogists 65
mycologists 26

N
neuropharmacologists 70

O
oceanographers 57–60
ornithologists 81

P
paleontologists 41, 61–64
petroleum geologists 41
petroleum technicians 43, 67
petrologists 65–68
pharmacologists 69–72
physical oceanographers 58
physicists 73–76

planetary astronomers 13
plant cytologists 26
plant geneticists 26

R
radio astronomers 13
research geneticists 37

S
seismologists 45
soil conservation technicians 78
soil scientists 77–80
solar astronomers 13
stellar astronomers 13

T
theoretical physicists 73
toxicologists 26, 29–30

Z
zoologists 21, 81–84

Browse and Learn More

Books

Burnie, David. *Eyewitness: Life.* New York: DK Publishing, 1999.

Farndon, John. *How the Earth Works.* Pleasantville, N.Y.: Reader's Digest, 1992.

Macaulay, David. *The New Way Things Work.* New York: Houghton Mifflin, 1998.

Orenstein, Ronald. *New Animal Discoveries.* Magic Attic Press, 2001.

Potter, Jean. *Science in Seconds for Kids: Over 100 Experiments You Can Do in 10 Minutes or Less.* Hoboken, N.J.: John Wiley and Sons, 1995.

Powledge, Fred. *Pharmacy in the Forest: How Medicines Are Found in the Natural World.* New York: Atheneum, 1998.

Pratt, Kristin Joy. *A Walk in the Rainforest.* Nevada City, Calif.: Dawn Publications, 1992.

Rey, H. A. *The Stars: A New Way to See Them.* New York: Mariner Books, 1976.

Roxbee Cox, Phil. *Atoms and Molecules.* Tulsa, Okla.: EDC Publications, 1993.

VanCleave, Janice. *Janice VanCleave's Earth Science for Every Kid: 101 Experiments That Really Work.* Hoboken, N.J.: John Wiley and Sons, 1991.

Websites

Cool Science for Curious Kids
http://www.hhmi.org/coolscience

For Kids Only: Earth Science Enterprise
http://kids.mtpe.hq.nasa.gov

Hotlist: Kids Did This in Science
http://sln.fi.edu/tfi/hotlists/kid-sci.html

Kids World: Science around the World
http://www.northvalley.net/kids/science.shtml

National Aquarium in Baltimore
http://www.aqua.org

National Geographic Kids
http://www.nationalgeographic.com/ngkids

Science Fair Central
http://school.discovery.com/sciencefaircentral

Science Made Simple
http://www.sciencemadesimple.com

Sci4Kids
http://www.ars.usda.gov/is/kids

Smithsonian National Museum of Natural History
http://www.mnh.si.edu/

Yes Mag: Canada's Science Magazine for Kids
http://www.yesmag.bc.ca

Yuckiest Site on the Internet
http://www.yucky.com